all recipes®
.com

tried & true

thanksgiving & christmas

top 200 recipes

all recipes®
.com

tried & true

thanksgiving
& christmas

top 200 recipes

Published by Allrecipes.com, Inc.
3317 3rd Ave. S., Suite D, Seattle, WA 98134
(206) 292-3990

For distribution information, contact Allrecipes.

Printed and bound in Canada.
Third Edition January 2006

Library of Congress Control Number: 2002015516

10 9 8 7 6 5 4 3

ISBN 0-9711-7233-1

SERIES EDITOR: Tim Hunt
EDITOR: Syd Carter
FOOD EDITOR: Jennifer Anderson
PRODUCTION MANAGER: Jill Charing
RECIPE EDITORS: Emily Brune, Richard Kozel, Britt Swearingen
ART DIRECTOR: Yann Oehl
DESIGNER: Jeff Cummings

Cover photograph copyright 2002, TRG Studios

Recipe shown on cover: *Rosemary Roasted Turkey* (81)
and *Carrot Souffle* (146)

dedication

· ·

This book is dedicated to all the people who gather family and friends together at their tables for the holidays.

acknowledgments

The book you are holding is a community cookbook: the recipes within come from the community of cooks who gather online at Allrecipes.com. It is the members of this community, first and foremost, who we would like to thank - anyone that has shared, reviewed, requested, or tried an Allrecipes recipe. The success of the Allrecipes community resides in your experience, enthusiasm, and generosity.

In addition, a huge debt of thanks is owed to the staff of Allrecipes - the people who have dedicated themselves to building a helpful, supportive environment for our community.

table of contents

introduction

What's your fondest holiday memory? Decorating sugar cookies with Mom? Savoring left-over turkey sandwiches with Dad? Tumbling in from the snow to be greeted by the sweet, spicy aroma of mulled cider? Likely you can recall dozens of holiday moments that make you sigh with contentment - and we"re sure that food plays a role in most of them.

Of course, the season is really all about being together with family and friends, and enjoy-ing traditions that bring you closer. However, the emphasis on food at Thanksgiving and Christmas can feel like a mixed blessing. There's the anticipation of special once-a-year treats, lavish spreads and a calendar full of parties to host and attend. But for those of us who do the majority of the holiday cooking, there's also a tremendous pressure to perform; to crank out delightful dishes at a rapid pace, and have it all look, smell and taste fabulous. But don't worry: millions of home cooks have been here before you, and they're sharing their very best, foolproof holiday recipes. These dishes are now yours for the taking! Traditional roast turkey and prime rib feasts with all the trimmings sit festively alongside favorite party foods, classic desserts, candies, edible gifts - and, of course, cookies!

With this invaluable collection of recipes, you've got one less thing to worry about during the holidays. In addition to recipes, you'll also find menu suggestions and plenty of detailed hints and tips written by our staff of cooking and baking experts. Go ahead and plan that cocktail party, potluck, cookie exchange party or caroling expedition. While you're at it, vol-unteer to host Thanksgiving dinner and Christmas, too. We'll get you through the season with flying colors!

Happy Holidays,
The Staff at Allrecipes

getting organized

The Thanksgiving and Christmas holidays are a special time of year set aside for gathering family and friends to enjoy good food and good company. Yet this precious time seems to fly by in a blur of swarming shopping malls, billowing clouds of flour and sugar, and roaring vacuum cleaners. It really is possible to enjoy your holiday celebrations instead of rushing madly about the kitchen from dawn until dusk; all it takes is some careful planning, and we're here to help!

getting organized

Thanksgiving and Christmas are a time for enjoying family, friends, and tradition, as well as a time for breaking out your most impressive and beloved recipes. Yet, just as you can count on the holidays being a time of joy and celebration, you can bet they're going to be hectic as well! Take some time to plan ahead and make this special season more enjoyable for everyone.

one month in advance

· Plan your menu and make a note of which items you'd like your guests to bring. Now is a good time to decide if you want to stick with traditional favorites, wow your guests with a unique menu that brings out the best in your culinary skills, or prepare an exciting blend of old and new.

· Extend written or verbal invitations, depending on how formal the occasion. When guests ask if they can bring anything, say yes, and consider sharing a few of your menu ideas with them.

· Pre-order your turkey, roast, duck, or ham. Don't miss out on the best selection by waiting until the last minute.

· Purchase all necessary supplies for food gifts: 1-quart or 1-liter jars for all those "cookie mixes in a jar" you'll be passing out on Christmas Eve; tins for mailing sweet treats around the country; and plenty of packing and shipping supplies. While you're at it, don't forget extra cooking gadgets for stocking stuffers!

two weeks in advance

· Confirm your guest list, as well as the menu items your guests have agreed to bring.

· Put out your favorite place settings, and form a general idea of where everyone is going to sit and your preferred serving style (a seated dinner, a buffet, a combination of both). Now is a good time to polish the silver and shine the crystal, if necessary.

· Make sure you have enough table space and chairs. If not, arrange to borrow or rent extra.

· Start making lists! No professional chef would dream of working without a checklist, and for this big occasion, neither should you. Make a thorough shopping list, and note every dish and serving piece you will need. If you're including wine, consider the type that will go best with your meal. Your lists might also include:

- Napkins, tablecloths, centerpieces, place settings
- Roasting pans and racks, carving knives and forks, basters, aluminum foil, plastic wrap
- Pots and pans
- Serving utensils and dishes
- A gravy boat and ladle
- Glasses for water, wine, cider, coffee, as well as pitchers and sugar bowls

the week of the big meal

- Clean out the refrigerator to make room for the groceries and prepared dishes to come.
- If you're buying a frozen turkey, think about how much time you'll need for thawing. For each five pounds of turkey, allow 24 hours of thaw time in the refrigerator (i.e., a 15-pound bird will take three full days).
- Prepare pastry for pies and refrigerate in plastic wrap.
- Prepare sauces, jellies, and dressings.
- Assemble the dishes you'd like to prepare in advance and then freeze or refrigerate. This will be your biggest timesaver and stress reliever on the day of the meal. Don't forget to consider thaw time, as well as the space you have available for freezing and refrigerating.
- Make your cakes, pies, and cookies.
- Determine when and where to serve each dish - remember to keep cool dishes cool and hot dishes hot!

a day before the meal

· Pre-chop vegetables.

· Prepare anything that needs to marinate overnight.

· Assemble appetizers and side dishes.

· Be sure you'll have enough room in the dishwasher and sink for the oncoming barrage of dirty dishes by putting away everything you won't need for the meal.

the big day!

This is when you reap the rewards of all your meticulous planning and preparation. You'll still be busy, but knowing you don't need to worry about having enough salad forks or baking an extra batch of cookies will make all the difference in the world. Here are some of the tasks you will want to save until the day of the meal:

· Reheat all the dishes you've frozen or refrigerated.

· Cook the turkey, roast, or other main dish.

· Prepare mashed potatoes and gravy.

· Warm breads and rolls.

· Arrange appetizers on serving platters.

· Prepare cider and coffee.

Your oven and microwave may be working overtime, but you can take comfort in knowing that you're just a few minutes away from enjoying a wonderful holiday meal with the people you love.

the aftermath

Once the feast has ended and your dinner guests have wandered from the table in a state of food-induced bliss, the daunting reality of dirty dishes and piles of leftovers sets in! It's time to let your organization and planning skills help you whip the scene into shape!

What would the holidays be without one of the most eagerly anticipated traditions of all - holiday leftovers? Some may wince at the thought of a week's-worth of turkey sandwiches and tired casseroles, but with a bit of forethought - and plenty of storage space - you can make the "meals after the meal" a delicious reminder of your culinary prowess.

Seemingly minor advance steps will make a big difference once the clean up process has begun. An already-emptied dishwasher will take care of dirty dishes in a hurry, and a pre-cleaned refrigerator will prove a welcome abode for your leftovers. Have enough clean containers ready so they can be filled at once, and keep freezer bags on hand for any items you may wish to store for the long term. Aluminum foil, plastic wrap, and wax paper are essential.

To put your leftovers to good use, you must handle them carefully. Immediately remove stuffing from the turkey, and refrigerate it separately. Slice up leftover meat, seal in aluminum foil or airtight containers, and refrigerate within two hours of cooking. Not only will this preserve precious space in your refrigerator, it will help the meat get to a safe storage temperature much more quickly. Bacteria forms rapidly in cooked meats, so it's essential to get them chilled if you wish to use them later! Transfer leftover sides to smaller dishes or containers. Refrigerated leftovers should be eaten within two or three days. Frozen leftovers will retain their quality for a month or two, and should be stored as airtight as possible. Label and date your freezer bags, and always thaw frozen items, especially meats, in the refrigerator or microwave.

Putting your leftovers to use is a great way to exercise your creativity! Leftover turkey is wonderful in soups and casseroles, and can bring new life to your favorite pasta dish. Diced ham makes an excellent addition to a salad. Sweet potatoes and mashed potatoes can be wrapped in tortillas and served with beans and cheese for an exciting change. Leftover rolls and bread can be used for sandwiches, or dried and transformed into croutons or bread pudding. Combinations of turkey, stuffing, potatoes, and gravy can be turned into tasty casseroles. Leftover cranberry sauce is a great way to liven up the classic turkey sandwich. How about turkey meatloaf, a stir-fry with succulent ham tossed in, or rice tossed with leftover vegetables? Let you imagination run wild!

You can find recipes to creatively reshape your leftovers on our website.
http://allrecipes.com/directory/1695.asp

menus

The holiday season holds one celebration after another. Whether you are having loved ones join you for dinner, a cocktail party, or a two-week stay, there are lots of fabulous menu ideas to choose from. Full of tips on timing and planning, these menus will serve as a guideline for your most important occasions. Parties, formal dinners, breakfasts, or entertaining children can be a lot of work, so we've done our best to help you organize the meal planning for this important time of year.

menus

old-fashioned turkey dinner

A golden roast turkey with all the trimmings is the order of the day. Tradition never tasted so good!

the week before…

Make the Oranged Cranberry Sauce, and refrigerate. Prepare and partially bake the Butterhorn Rolls; freeze. See our Dinner Roll tips, page 44.

a day before…

Prepare the Savory Turkey Gravy (use the turkey giblets for the stock). Roast garlic for the mashed potatoes, and refrigerate. Prepare and refrigerate the Awesome Sausage, Apple and Dried Cranberry Stuffing. Bake and mash the sweet potatoes, and refrigerate. Prepare the Make-Ahead Mashed Potatoes, and place in a serving dish (do not bake); refrigerate. Bake the Brown Family's Favorite Pumpkin Pie, and store at room temperature.

the big day…

Reheat stuffing in microwave or oven until warm, but not hot. Stuff turkey, and roast. See our Roast Turkey tips, page 32. Assemble the Favorite Green Bean Casserole and Gourmet Sweet Potato Classic. Bake the Make-Ahead Mashed potatoes. Take advantage of the fact that the turkey needs to stand about 30 minutes before carving, and use the time to bake the sweet potatoes and green bean casserole. Reheat the gravy and the rolls just before serving.

cajun turkey dinner

A spicy, juicy, crisp-skinned turkey is the centerpiece of this Southern menu. You don't even need to be Cajun to make this a part of your family's favorite holiday rituals!

the week before…

Prepare and refrigerate the Baked Cranberry Sauce. Prepare and partially bake the Angel Biscuits II; freeze. See our Dinner Roll tips, page 44.

a day before…

Make the Savory Turkey Gravy, and store it in the refrigerator. Bake the cornbread for the stuffing. Bake the Pecan Pie, and store it at room temperature.

the big day…

Heat the oil for frying the turkey. See our Fried Turkey tips, page 33.

Prepare Southern Candied Sweet Potatoes, Apple Pecan Corn Bread Dressing, Cheesy Green Beans, and Corn Pudding V; assemble these dishes as much as possible in the morning, and begin cooking after you have immersed the bird in the hot oil.

Take advantage of the fact that the turkey needs to stand about 30 minutes before carving, and use the time to reheat the gravy and biscuits.

prime rib feast

You can't go wrong with a magnificent prime rib roast at the head of your Christmas dinner table. With our easy recipes, the meal is guaranteed to be a smashing success.

- Prime Rib . . . . page 88
- Roasted Garlic Mashed Potatoes . . . . page 122
- Fresh Herb Dinner Rolls . . . . page 109
- Brussels Sprouts in Mustard Sauce . . . . page 144
- Butternut Squash with Onions and Pecans . . . . page 136
- Eggnog Cheesecake . . . . page 168

the week before…

Prepare and partially bake the Fresh Herb Dinner Rolls; freeze. See our Dinner Roll tips, page 44.

a day before…

Bake the Eggnog Cheesecake, and chill in the refrigerator. See our Cheesecake tips, page 48.

the big day…

Cook the Prime Rib. See our Prime Rib tips, page 35. Cook the Butternut Squash with Pecans and Onions and the Brussels Sprouts in Mustard Sauce. Boil potatoes for Roasted Garlic Mashed Potatoes. The roast needs to stand for 15 or 20 minutes before carving; reheat the rolls during this time, and finish preparing the mashed potatoes.

holiday ham dinner

Get ready for exclamations of delight when this lovely feast unfolds at the holiday table.

a day before…

Bake the Chocolate Plum Pudding Cake, and refrigerate. Cook, cool, and refrigerate the Baked Sweet Potatoes with Ginger and Honey.

the big day…

Prepare and bake the Tangy Honey Glazed Ham. See our Ham tips, page 37. Prepare Lemon Pepper Green Beans; refrigerate until ready to cook. Assemble and bake the Corn Casserole. Make the biscuit dough. Cook the green beans, reheat the sweet potatoes, and bake the biscuits.

roast duck

The rich flavors and elegant presentation of this roast duck are perfect for a stylish Christmas meal. One (4 pound) duck will serve four people.

the week before...

Prepare the Apricot Cranberry Chutney, and store it in the refrigerator. Prepare and partially bake Colleen's Potato Crescent Rolls; freeze. See our Dinner Roll Tips, page 44.

a day before...

Prepare and refrigerate the dressing for the Roast Duck with Apple Dressing. Chop the vegetables for the Roasted Vegetables, seal them in plastic, and refrigerate. Bake the Cranberry Apple Pie.

the big day...

Dress the duck, and begin roasting about 90 minutes before it is to be served. The Roasted Vegetables may be placed on a separate shelf in the oven during the final 40 minutes the duck is roasting, or use a larger baking pan and arrange the vegetables around the duck. Set out the chutney and carve the duck while you reheat the rolls.

holiday cocktail party

Put on your Christmas best and have friends and neighbors over for a soiree they'll remember long after the holidays are over. One warning: with a spread like this, they may never want to go home!

- Artichoke and Roasted Red Pepper Dip . . . . page 54
- Chutney Baked Brie . . . . page 58
- Rockin' Oysters Rockefeller . . . . page 63
- Marbled Pumpkin Cheesecake . . . . page 167
- Raspberry Truffle Fudge . . . . page 208
- Cranberry Pistachio Biscotti . . . . page 225
- Luscious Eggnog . . . . page 68
- Christmas Punch . . . . page 75
- Assorted Fresh Vegetables
- Bread

the week before…

Prepare the Raspberry Truffle Fudge and the Pistachio Cranberry Biscotti. Keep the fudge refrigerated, and store the biscotti in a cookie tin.

a day before…

Prepare and refrigerate the Artichoke and Roasted Red Pepper Dip. Bake the Marbled Pumpkin Cheesecake; cover, and refrigerate. Prepare and chill the Luscious Eggnog and Christmas Punch.

the big day…

Assemble the Chutney Baked Brie and boil oysters and prepare sauce for the Rockin' Oysters Rockefeller. Refrigerate both appetizers until ready to bake. Slice vegetables and bread to serve with the dip. A couple of large bowls filled with ice may be used to keep the eggnog and punch chilled.

caroling party

Gather kids of all ages to warm up their voices and spread Christmas cheer around the neighborhood; then bring them back to warm their tummies with these tasty treats.

the week before…

Prepare the Cocoa Rum Balls and Gingerbread Men, and store them in cookie tins.

a day before…

Bake Santa's Favorite Cake, and keep it fresh inside a sealed container.

the day of the party…

Prepare and refrigerate the Pumpkin Dip and Cheese Ball.

during the party…

Assemble the Stuffed Mushrooms IV and the cheese mixture for the Bread Pot Fondue. Form the bread pot. Before the caroling activities begin, roll the Rum Balls in confectioner's sugar, and set them out along with the Gingerbread Man and the cake. The dip and Cheese Ball can be left in the refrigerator until ready to serve. Heat the Stuffed Mushrooms and prepare the Hot Spiced Cider during the party. If you'll only be caroling for an hour, you may want to fill the bread pot and stick it in the oven while you are out! Otherwise, stick it in the oven when you return, and enjoy the other treats while it's toasting.

holiday brunch

Whether it's a weekend get-together with friends or a house full of guests to feed, this (mostly) make-ahead brunch menus will start the day off right.

the week before…

Assemble and freeze the Christmas Breakfast Sausage. Bake Sour Cream Coffee Cake III; cool completely and double wrap in plastic wrap.

a day before…

Prepare the Cranberry Waldorf. Thaw the casserole in the refrigerator.

in the morning…

Stick the casserole in the oven. Wrap coffee cake in foil, and reheat in oven while casserole is baking; remove from oven when warm. Make the Candy Cane Cocoa. Stir the Cranberry Waldorf just before serving.

cooking basics

On the following pages, you'll find tips for preparing, cooking, and presenting holiday favorites. Hone your baking and cooking skills with our handy, step-by-step instructions for everything from roasting turkey to mashing potatoes to kneading dinner rolls. We've even included the secrets to making the perfect cheesecake.

cooking basics

starters

Eating officially begins when the first appetizers are served. Your selection can set the tone for the meal that follows. The right presentation and garnish can elevate the simplest dip to a stylish hors d'oeuvre sure to please the eye and the palate.

presentation

Presentation begins with the serving dish. Some of the best and most beautiful containers come from Mother Nature herself. Hollowed out cabbages and squash make perfect bowls for savory dips and spreads - or use them to hold vegetable crudités. Lemon and orange cups also make attractive small containers for sweet or savory dips and spreads. Hollowed-out bread loaves in different sizes and shapes can be filled with warm dips that you bake in the oven. Other good containers included baskets, decorative trays and platters, fancy cutting boards, unique bowls in different shapes, sizes, and colors.

garnish

For that perfect garnish, look to the world of herbs and spices. Fresh thyme, chives, lavender flowers, and the ubiquitous parsley will add beautiful and edible touches to your appetizer trays. When it comes to spices, just a sprinkle of paprika, curry powder, or cinnamon is sure to add punch to stuffed eggs, dips, and spreads. Also consider citrus zest, sprinklings of seeds like cumin, caraway, or black sesame, Parmesan cheese shavings, or tiny, elegant fruits to embellish your hors d'oeuvres. Sweet appetizers can be dressed up with a simple dusting of confectioner's sugar or cocoa powder. Just remember to keep all the garnishes simple; often, a single green leaf or bright sprig of herb is all you need to wow the eye.

tips

- Place only one or two different kinds of appetizers on each serving tray. Having a jumble of different munchies confuses the eye and can make it difficult for your guests to choose which ones they want to sample.

- Make sure there are plenty of receptacles for garbage; nobody wants to see piles of tooth-picks, olive pits or shrimp tails scattered throughout the serving tables and the room.

- Don't make appetizers too large. They should be able to be eaten in one or two delicious bites.

- Offer a variety of tastes, textures, and colors. Avoid serving only fussy, intricate little appetizers, which can mask each other's beauty. Throw in some less delicate creations like dips, spreads, or pâtés. Not only will this cut down on the work of preparing individual appetizers, but it will also emphasize the unique qualities of every dish you are serving.

the main course

The main course is the centerpiece of the holiday meal, and requires careful planning. Everything you need to know is right here at your fingertips - from how much to plan per person to exact cooking instructions.

turkey

Your first decision will be selecting between a fresh or frozen turkey. A fresh bird is more expensive, but will save you time and precious refrigerator space since you'll be buying the bird the day before you wish to roast it. Remember to reserve your turkey with the butcher to ensure you get the size you want. Count on 1¼ pounds per person, or more if you want leftovers.

A frozen turkey needs to be defrosted. The preferred method is to defrost it on a tray in the refrigerator. Allow one day for every five pounds (i.e., a 15-pound turkey will require three days to defrost thoroughly). An alternate method is to defrost the bird in a cold-water bath. Leave the turkey in its original wrapping, place in the sink or in a clean bucket, and cover completely with cold tap water. Change the water every 30 minutes, allowing 30 minutes per pound to thaw (i.e., a 15-pound turkey will take approximately 7½ hours). It's also possible to use a combination of these methods.

roast turkey

Roasting is the most familiar and popular way to cook the turkey. When you're ready to roast, remove the giblets, rinse the bird inside and out, and pat dry with paper towels. If you are stuffing the turkey, do so now. Remember to stuff loosely, allowing about ½ to ¾ cup per pound of bird. Place turkey on a rack in a roasting pan and brush the skin with melted butter or oil. Tuck the drumsticks under the folds of skin or tie together with string. Lastly, insert a meat thermometer into the thickest part of the thigh. The thermometer should point towards the body, and should not touch the bone. Place the turkey in an oven preheated to 350 degrees F (175 degrees C). Bake until the skin is a light golden color, and then cover loosely with a foil "tent" to prevent the skin from burning. During the last 45 minutes of cooking, remove the foil to brown the skin. Basting is not necessary, but will promote even browning.

The best test to determine if the turkey is done is the temperature of the meat, not the color of the skin. The turkey is cooked when the thigh meat reaches an internal temperature of 180 degrees F (85 degrees C), and when the breast meat reaches an internal temperature of 170 degrees F (75 degrees C). If your turkey has been stuffed, it is important to check the temperature of the stuffing; it should be 165 degrees F (70 degrees C). When the turkey is done, remove from the oven and allow to stand for 30 minutes. Use the chart below to estimate cooking time.

Weight of Bird	Roasting Time (Unstuffed)	Roasting Time (Stuffed)
10 to 18 pounds	3 to 3½ hours	3¾ to 4½ hours
15 to 22 pounds	3½ to 4 hours	4½ to 5 hours
22 to 24 pounds	4 to 4½ hours	5 to 5½ hours
24 to 29 pounds	4½ to 5 hours	5½ to 6¼ hours

fried turkey

Deep-frying a whole turkey is a Cajun tradition that produces sensationally juicy meat and delightfully crispy skin. An added advantage of cooking a turkey this way is that it takes less than an hour to cook the whole bird! It also frees up your oven for other dishes.

Don't attempt to fry a turkey without the right tools. You'll need a heavy-duty portable propane burner and a very large stockpot (26 to 40 quart capacity) or a custom-made turkey-frying pot. The process also requires a contraption that will help you SAFELY lower the turkey into a vat of boiling oil, and remove it SAFELY once the turkey is done. Buy a tool specially designed for this purpose. Have several well-insulated potholders or oven mitts available, and safety goggles to protect your eyes from oil splatters. Keep an all-purpose fire extinguisher nearby. Finally, you'll need a candy thermometer for measuring the temperature of the oil.

The ideal turkey size for deep-frying is between 10 and 15 pounds; anything larger will be difficult to handle. If you're feeding lots of people, it's better to prepare two turkeys rather than attempt to cook one bird. The turkey should be fresh or completely thawed before cooking. Trim the neck skin until you have at least a two-inch opening so the frying oil can flow freely through the cavity. If the bird has a plastic pop-up doneness indicator, remove it.

To determine how much oil you'll need, place the bird in the pot you intend to use for frying. Pour in cold water until the turkey is covered by a couple of inches. There should still be several inches between the surface of the water and the top of the pot. If there's not, you need a bigger pot. Now, remove the turkey and pat it dry with paper towels. Measure the water that's in the pot: this is how much oil you'll need, so make a note of it, then wash and dry the pot. To be genuinely Cajun, you'll want to use peanut oil for frying the bird. It's expensive, but gives the best flavor and will not smoke when it gets hot the way some other oils will.

Deep-frying a whole turkey is a messy proposition, and presents some hazards, so it's always done outdoors on a flat surface. Wear old clothes that you don't mind getting spattered with oil. Long-sleeve shirts, long pants, and shoes that completely cover your feet are highly recommended. Clear all children, pets and other flammable or well-loved material far away from the frying area. Pat your seasoned bird with paper towels until completely dry. (Water and hot oil do not mix, and you don't want to be burned by flying 400 degree oil.) Allow the bird to come to room temperature. Bring out a big tray with several layers of paper bags on it. This is where the turkey will land and drain when it's done.

Pour the desired amount of oil into the pot and fire up the burner. Stick a candy thermometer in the pot: once it reaches 400 degrees F (205 degrees C), you're ready. Turn off the burner momentarily so that any splattered oil will not cause flare-ups. Slowly lower the turkey partway into the oil. The oil will bubble up fiercely. Pause momentarily until it subsides. Repeat the process, lowering gradually until the turkey is completely submerged and resting on the bottom of the pot. Now you can turn the burner on again. If the oil had a chance to cool down to below 350 degrees F (175 degrees C), crank it up high until the oil returns to 350 degrees F (175 degrees C), and then turn down the burner to maintain the temperature.

Allow 3 to 3½- minutes of cooking time per pound of turkey. This means a 15-pound turkey will take about 45 minutes to cook. To check for doneness, turn off the burner and call your assistant to help you pull the turkey partway out of the pot and insert a meat thermometer into the thigh. When it reads 180 degrees F (82 degrees C), your bird is done! Raise the turkey out of the pot and let the oil drip from it for a minute. Make sure the cavity drains. Carefully place it on the tray you covered with paper bags and let it drain for a few minutes longer, until the turkey is cool enough to transfer to a serving platter.

carving a turkey

Once the bird is done cooking, it should stand for 20 to 35 minutes, depending on its size. This gives the juices a chance to soak back into the flesh, allowing for succulent cuts of meat. Before you begin carving, have a warm serving platter ready and waiting.

Arrange the turkey, breast side up, on a cutting board. Steady the turkey with a carving fork while slicing. Using a sharp knife, slice through the meat between the breast and the leg. Next, using a large knife as an aid, press the thigh outward to find the hip joint. Slice down through the joint and remove the leg. Cut between the thighbone and drumstick bone to divide the leg into one thigh piece and one drumstick. To carve the drumstick, cut a thick slice of meat from one side, along the bone. Next, turn the drumstick over so that the cut side faces down. Cut off another thick slice of meat. Repeat, turning the drumstick onto a flat side and cutting off meat, carving a total of four thick slices. To slice the thigh, place it flat side down on a cutting board. Cut parallel to the bone and slice off the meat. Place all the cuts on the warmed serving platter as you work.

Before you carve the breast, the wings must be removed. Slice diagonally down through the edge of the breast toward the wing. Using a knife as an aid, press the wing out to find the shoulder joint; cut through the joint and remove the wing. Place the wing on the serving platter as-is.

To carve the breast meat, hold the back of the carving fork against the breastbone. Starting parallel to the breastbone, slice diagonally through the meat. Lift off each slice, holding it between the knife and fork, and place on the warm serving platter. Continue until you have carved all the meat on one side of the breast. Repeat, carving the other side of breast.

prime rib

A rib roast (a.k.a., prime rib, or standing rib roast) is a magnificent centerpiece for any special-occasion meal. This cut of beef is highly prized: it is meltingly tender, unbelievably juicy, and boasts a bold, beefy flavor that needs no fancy embellishments.

Shopping for a roast can be confusing, though. The very same cut of meat is often called by different names. "Prime rib" is the most famous moniker for this cut, but the word "prime" actually describes the grade of the meat, not the cut. The top three grades of beef are Prime, Choice, and Select. Meats graded 'Prime' are sold almost exclusively to restaurants - so while you may have eaten Prime rib in a restaurant on occasion, you probably won't be able to buy a prime rib roast at the grocery store. Instead, look for a Choice cut by the name of "rib roast," "eye of the rib roast," or "standing rib roast." A rib roast can be boneless, in which case it may be called an eye of the rib roast, or, it can have the ribs still attached, in which case it may be called a standing rib roast. The meat will be more flavorful if you roast it with the ribs still attached, but a boneless roast is definitely easier to carve; the choice is up to you. If you do buy a roast with attached ribs, make sure the butcher removes the chine bone (the backbone) first, or the roast will be difficult to carve.

You can count on the fact that most people at your table are going to want big servings of this mouthwatering roast, so allow at least six ounces of cooked, trimmed meat per adult. A boneless roast will give you about two 6-ounce servings per pound, and a bone-in roast will give you one to one-and-a-half servings.

You'll be glad to know that once you've picked out a roast, your work is half done; rib roast doesn't need a marinade or any complicated preparations. If you like, prepare a simple seasoning rub: fresh herbs, lemon zest, garlic, pepper and Dijon mustard are all good matches for beef. To infuse even more flavor into the meat, insert slivers of garlic into tiny slits in the roast. You can cover the meat with the spice rub up to 24 hours in advance, wrap it tightly with plastic wrap and refrigerate until you're ready to roast. Don't salt the roast until right before cooking.

Place the meat in a roasting pan that's not much bigger than the roast itself. If the pan is too big, the juices from the meat will spread out and evaporate. For a boneless roast, use a roasting rack. If you've chosen a bone-in roast, the bones themselves will serve as your roasting rack. One side of the meat will have more fat on it; you'll want this side facing up so the meat will baste itself as it cooks.

You've splurged for an expensive cut of meat. If you don't already own one, spend a few more dollars on a meat thermometer; it's the very best way to guarantee that your roast turns out exactly the way you want it. For an accurate reading, push the thermometer into the middle of the roast, making sure the tip is not touching fat or bone. We recommend you cook this cut of meat to medium-rare (130-140 degrees F/55-60 degrees C) or medium (145-155 degrees F/63-68 degrees C). The slices taken from the ends of the roast will be the most done, and the middle will be the least done, so you should be able to suit the preferences of everyone at the table. Serve with pan drippings and horseradish on the side. Remember that the roast's temperature will rise at least five degrees after you remove it from the oven. Let the roast stand for 15 or 20 minutes before carving to let the juices reabsorb.

ham

There are three basic varieties: city ham, country ham, and fresh ham. The one you are most likely to encounter in the grocery store is city ham, which has been soaked in brine and then either smoked or boiled. City ham is moist and tender, and its flavor ranges from mild and salty to rich and smoky, depending on how it has been cooked. Country-cured ham is made from a pig that has been fed fruits and nuts to produce more flavorful meat. These hams are dry-cured by packing them in salt, then are smoked over a bed of fragrant hardwoods and hung in a cool place to be aged for at least 60 days (although some are aged up to seven years). Country-cured ham has a more intense flavor, but is drier than brined ham, since the long aging process causes more water to evaporate from the meat. Rarely will you encounter a fresh ham, a type of uncured pork that - unlike city and country ham - must be fully cooked before eating.

Ham with the bone left in tends to be more flavorful than a boneless ham. Bone-in hams are also more decorative, and make for a more ceremonious presentation on special occasions. Many brands of bone-in ham are spiral-cut. This means that the ham has been carved in a continuous spiral all the way around the bone, producing thin slices that easily peel away, making the ham very easy to serve. If you do choose a bone-in ham, take the weight of the bone into account when deciding what size to buy. If the ham has a large bone, you will need to count on at least ¾ pound for each person; with a boneless ham, count on at least ¼ pound per person.

The most traditional way to prepare a whole ham is to bake it. First, read the label to determine if your ham has been partially cooked or fully cooked. A partially-cooked ham requires about 20 minutes per pound in a moderate (350 degrees F/175 degrees C) oven. A fully - cooked ham will require about 10 minutes per pound in order to be heated all the way through. A meat thermometer comes in very handy for baking hams: when the internal temperature reaches 160 degrees F (80 degrees C), it's ready.

Although ham is perfectly delicious all by itself, you can make it extra-special by adding a glaze. The most popular glaze recipes contain combinations of fruit juice, wine or whiskey, honey, mustard, brown sugar, fruit preserves, and spices. Place the ham cut-side down in a baking pan and brush it with some glaze. If the ham is going to be in the oven for more than an hour, you may also want to place a foil "tent" over it in order to keep the meat from drying out. Continue to brush the ham with glaze and baste it with the pan juices every 20 minutes or so, until heated through. To finish the ham and give it a delicious caramelized coating, remove the foil tent, brush it with glaze and pan juices one more time, then turn your oven to the broiler setting. Allow the outside of the ham to brown nicely - this should only take about five minutes, but watch it closely so it doesn't get too dark.

sides

Accessorizing your main dish is essential for adding that festive feeling to your feast. A meal would not be a celebration without the adornment of plenty of special-occasion side dishes. Indulge yourself for the holidays, and generously set the table with all sorts of savory selections. Show off with a sweet, brightly colored yam casserole served alongside velvety mashed potatoes. Delight your fellow feasters with a new twist on the traditional, or master one of the classics with these simple tips.

Looking for an easy way to round out the holiday meal? Steamed vegetables are quick, healthy, and add plenty of color and variety to standard entertaining fare. The microwave is perfect for steaming vegetables - you can even cook them in the same dish you use to serve them. All you need to do is add a small amount of water to the bottom of the dish, cover with a lid or a piece of plastic wrap (just be sure to leave a little room for the steam to escape) and microwave on high for four to eight minutes, depending on the thickness of the vegetables. Dress up your veggies for the occasion by tossing them with cooked, crumbled bacon, caramelized onions, toasted or candied nuts, or a sprinkle of flavorful cheese such as gorgonzola or Parmesan.

gravy

Making gravy is basic chemistry. Dislike lumps? Keep this in mind: gravy only becomes lumpy when flour particles stick together. This can be avoided by cooking a fat (such as clarified butter, vegetable oil or pan drippings) together with an equal proportion of flour - a combination which is known as a roux and serves as a thickener for gravy. As a general rule, ½ cup of roux will thicken 4 cups of liquid. Any type of liquid can be added to a roux to make gravy. Here's a how-to guide for making turkey gravy using turkey broth and drippings from a roasting pan.

- **Step 1:** In a heavy saucepan or skillet, whisk together ¼ cup all-purpose flour and ¼ cup meat fat, butter, or oil over low heat. Stir constantly until all flour particles are coated and the flour becomes golden in color. The cooking removes any raw flour taste and adds color to the gravy. Set aside and allow pan to cool.

- **Step 2:** Once the pan and roux have cooled, whisk in four cups hot broth and simmer over medium heat, stirring frequently for five minutes. (To prepare your own turkey broth, simmer the neck, giblets and gizzards for one hour in lightly salted water to cover. Strain and remove fat.)

- **Step 3:** To deglaze the roasting pan, begin by removing the cooked turkey and as much grease or fat as possible, using a spoon, ladle or gravy separator. Deglaze the pan by placing it over medium heat and adding ½ cup water or other liquid, such as wine or stock. Stir constantly and scrape the bottom of the pan to loosen browned bits. Simmer for one minute.

- **Step 4:** Pour the liquid from the roasting pan into the gravy base (the roux and the turkey stock), and cook until the mixture boils and thickens, stirring constantly, about five to eight minutes. Skim off any surface fat.

- **Step 5:** Season to taste with salt and pepper or fresh chopped sage. You've just made four cups of savory gravy!

mashed potatoes

Different types of potatoes yield different flavors and textures. For light, fluffy, slightly-mealy mashed potatoes, use a high-starch variety, such as the Russet (i.e., Idaho potatoes). For smooth and creamy mashed potatoes, use a high-moisture variety such as Yellow Finn or Yukon Gold.

For the best results, cut the potatoes into cubes of about ¾ inch (2 cm) square. Bring a pot of water to a boil, salt it generously, and add the potatoes. Keep the water at a heavy simmer, not a rolling boil, and begin checking for doneness after about 15 minutes. Under-cooked potatoes will be lumpy and pasty when you mash them, and over-cooked potatoes will be gluey, so watch carefully. Drain them as soon as they are soft and tender all the way through.

Now, be sure to mash those taters before they cool off! The best gadget for this task is a potato ricer, and the next best thing is a food mill. These two tools work well because the potatoes achieve a uniform texture as they pass through evenly sized holes. A traditional hand-held potato masher works passably, as you probably know from experience, but it demands that you mash the same potatoes over and over again in order to achieve smoothness. Doing so may cause you to smash open the swollen starch cells, resulting in gluey mashed potatoes. And unless you have a fondness for wallpaper paste, never, ever try to mash them in a food processor!

Next, mix in butter, milk, cream, seasonings, and any other additions that capture your imagination and your taste buds. It's preferable to have all of these ingredients warm or at room temperature before adding them to the potatoes, to avoid cooling them down. At this point, you can add smoothness and fluff by briefly whipping the potatoes with a mixer on its lowest speed. Keep those little starch cells in mind, though, and don't get overzealous, or the potatoes will turn runny on you. Now, pile them high in a serving dish and tell everyone to get 'em while they're hot!

sweet potatoes

The innate sweetness of sweet potatoes makes them a natural match for ingredients we usually associate with desserts, like brown sugar, vanilla, cinnamon, honey, maple syrup, ginger, coconut, nutmeg, pineapple, pecans, and fruit juices. For a quick, more savory side dish, peel and shred some sweet potatoes and saute them with a little butter or olive oil. Season simply with salt and pepper, and, perhaps, a splash of balsamic vinegar or a sprinkle of herbs or shredded cheese.

Choose sweet potatoes that are firm, with unwrinkled skin and no bruises or soft spots. Store them in a cool, dry place, or in a container that's open to the air. Never refrigerate raw sweet potatoes - they will develop a hard core in the middle and their flavor will deteriorate rapidly.

stuffing and dressing

Whether you call it "stuffing" or "dressing," this holiday side dish is always one of the stars of the dinner table.

For bread stuffing use a day-old loaf of firm or dense European-style bread instead of a soft white bread. Cornbread dressing is best made with home-baked golden cornbread. A couple pans of cornbread should be made at least a day in advance or weeks ahead and frozen. Cut the bread into cubes and allow them to air-dry overnight before proceeding.

Fruits, vegetables, and herbs make for flavorful additions to any stuffing. Since dried fruits are full of intense flavors and are able maintain their texture during hours of cooking, it makes them ideal for stuffing. Try dates, figs, prunes, cranberries, apples or cherries. Likewise, a variety of vegetables such as mushrooms, celery and onions make for flavorful stuffing ingredients. All vegetables should be precooked prior to incorporating in a stuffing recipe. And don't forget the herbs! Sage is a classic addition to stuffing, but rosemary, thyme and parsley are wonderful too.

A turkey can hold about one cup of stuffing per pound. Once prepared, toss the stuffing lightly with a fork to keep it light and airy. Loosely stuff the turkey cavity, as the dressing will expand slightly. Don't forget to stuff the neck cavity! Once stuffed, pull the neck skin up and pin it down with a skewer to enclose the opening. The body cavity opening may be trussed or sewed closed to protect exposed dressing, however a piece of aluminum foil placed over the opening with legs tied back also works well. Any extra stuffing should be placed in a buttered casserole dish, covered and refrigerated until ready to bake.

Never stuff a bird until right before you're ready to roast it, as the cavity can provide an environment for bacteria to grow. The stuffing should be warm when placed in the turkey so it reaches 165 degrees F (70 degrees C) by the time the bird is done. Remove the stuffing immediately and serve or refrigerate it. If the turkey is finished cooking before the stuffing has reached the correct temperature scoop it out, and place it in a greased baking dish. Microwave it on high or bake it at 350 degrees F (175 degrees C) until it reaches the correct temperature.

If you decide to bake your stuffing in a casserole dish rather than in a turkey, cover and bake it at 350 degrees F (175 degrees C) for 30 minutes or until it is heated to 165 degrees F (70 degrees C). For a crusty top, remove the lid during the last 15 minutes of cooking.

cranberry sauce

A dish of ruby-red homemade cranberry sauce will add a gorgeous touch to the dinner table. Cranberry sauce is surprisingly easy to make. Simply combine fresh or frozen whole cranberries with water, and add sugar to suit your taste. You can dress up the sauce with your favorite flavorings like cinnamon, nutmeg, cloves, orange zest, or ginger. Enhance it even more with other fruits such as peeled, chopped apples, raisins, or dried apricots. Substitute some or all of the water for orange juice, apple juice, brandy, or rum if you like. Simmer all the ingredients together over moderate heat. The sauce is ready when the cranberries pop!

gelatin salads

What would a holiday be without a glistening, shivering gelatin mold on the table? Here are hints on dressing up your gelatin for the occasion.

You can make gelatin desserts opaque and creamy with the addition of whipped cream, nondairy whipped topping, softened cream cheese, sour cream, cottage cheese or even mayonnaise. Before folding in your favorite addition, first prepare the gelatin as usual, and then chill it slightly. Beat in your additions until the mixture is smooth and evenly colored.

Add texture, flavor and visual appeal to any gelatin dessert by mixing in fruit, vegetables, nuts or marshmallows. Some of these things like to float, and some like to sink. However, it's possible to tame those morsels and make them stay put by waiting until the gelatin is semi-firm – about the consistency of cold egg whites – before pushing in the fruit.

Some fruits have naturally occurring enzymes that will break down the gelatin's structure, so that it will never get firm. The fruits to watch out for are pineapple, kiwi, figs, ginger, papaya, guava and mangoes. Cooking will break down the offending enzymes though, and since canned fruit has been cooked, it's safe to use any canned fruit in your gelatin, including canned pineapple.

For easy unmolding, spritz the pan lightly with cooking spray before pouring in the gelatin. Prepare the presentation plate by moistening it with water. This will make it easier for the gelatin mold to slide around a little so you can center it flawlessly. Now dunk the mold in warm water for about 10 seconds and loosen the edges with a table knife to break the vacuum. Invert the plate over the mold and flip! Lift the mold gently, at an angle. You should now have a perfectly formed shimmering sculpture of cool, fruity fun poised to win over every person seated at the dinner table.

baking

During the year, we're often too busy to embrace the joys of baking, but during the holidays, we feel more inspired to try a hand at grandmother's favorites. Pick a recipe that tantalizes your taste buds , and let the wonderful smells and flavors of home-baked holiday goods bring a festive flair to your kitchen! Here are a few simple tricks of the (baking) trade.

dinner rolls

There's no getting around the fact that making bread from scratch is more time-consuming than buying it, but there's just no comparison between rolls that come out of a plastic bag and rolls that come out of your very own oven.

You can use any yeast-bread recipe to prepare rolls. White or wheat, sour or sweet, whole grain or plain Jane, buttery dough or sourdough - if you can make it into a loaf, you can form it into a roll. And if you own a bread machine or a mixer with a dough hook, bread of all kinds is at your fingertips with just a little bit of measuring and the flip of a switch. Shape it, bake it, and you're done.

To divide a batch of dough into rolls, wait until the dough has risen once, then gently deflate it with your fist. On a clean surface, grab the dough in both hands and gently stretch it out into a log. Now use a pastry scraper (a.k.a. bench knife) or a stiff spatula to divide the log of dough into equal portions and shape each one into a round. Dust a baking sheet with flour and cover it with a sheet of plastic wrap. As you finish forming each dough round, place it under the plastic wrap to keep it from drying out.

As an alternative to regular round rolls, try making savory pinwheels. Once the dough has risen the first time, deflate it and roll it into a single rectangle about ½-inch thick. Spread the entire surface with butter and sprinkle it with herbs, seeds, nuts, and/or cheese. Roll it up jellyroll-style, seal the seam, and cut the log into slices. Allow the rolls to rise a second time and bake as usual. (This is the same method you would use for cinnamon rolls, replacing the herbs and cheese with brown sugar, cinnamon, raisins and/or nuts.)

If you're planning to serve rolls right away, allow the dough to rise a second time, until about double in size, and bake them. If you want to save the rolls for tomorrow, make sure you've wrapped the individual dough balls tightly in plastic and place them in the refrigerator. When you're ready, put them in a warm place, let them finish rising, then bake as usual.

Freezing the dough is also an option – perfect when you want to have fresh rolls in the weeks ahead. There are two ways you can go about this: once you have shaped the rolls, and before they rise a second time, put the covered pan in the freezer until the dough is frozen stiffly. Pop the frozen rolls into a heavy-duty, resealable plastic bag, and tuck them into the freezer until you're ready for them. To defrost, place the rolls on a tray dusted with flour and cover them with lightly greased plastic wrap. You can also freeze the shaped rolls by placing them in a well-greased, disposable aluminum baking pan and double-wrap them with foil or heavy plastic wrap. If you allow enough space between the rolls, you can thaw and bake them in the same pan. Use a permanent marker to note the correct oven temperature and baking time right on the plastic or foil. The frozen rolls will take a day to thaw in the refrigerator, or several hours at room temperature. Bread dough will keep in the freezer for up to a month.

When the rolls are fully risen and ready to go into the oven, consider adding some finishing touches. To make the tops shiny, golden and crispy, brush them with beaten egg, or coat them with melted butter to lend them a soft texture. Have some fun with toppings, too. Brush the rolls with the coating of your choice and sprinkle on seeds or nuts (try chopped walnuts, hazelnuts, pecans, pine nuts, sunflower seeds, poppy seeds, caraway seeds, or sesame seeds). A bit of grated cheese will melt and brown to a deliciously rich, crunchy crust – Parmesan, sharp Cheddar and mozzarella are especially good.

You can freeze bread loaves or rolls after they have been baked. Wait until they have cooled completely and make sure to double wrap them in plastic bags. When you want to reheat them, wrap the rolls in aluminum foil and reheat them in a moderate (350 degrees F/175 degrees C) oven.

quick breads

The term 'quick bread' refers to any bread that uses chemical leaveners (baking powder and/or baking soda) as opposed to yeast, and requires no kneading or rising time. This category includes all kinds of holiday favorites like pumpkin bread, cranberry-orange muffins, and cinnamon coffeecake. The real secret to perfectly moist, tender and well-shaped quick bread is to be scrupulously careful in your mixing. Combine the dry ingredients – flour, leavener, salt and spices – in one bowl and mix them thoroughly with a wire whisk. In another bowl, beat together the fat, sugar, and eggs in the order the recipe advises. Stir any other ingredients – fruit or fruit puree, nuts, flavorings – into the wet ingredients. Only when each bowl of ingredients is mixed thoroughly should they be combined. Pour the dry ingredients into the wet ones and fold them together gently by hand. Stir only until all the dry ingredients are moistened. Don't worry about a few lumps – they will disappear during baking.

Quick bread recipes are fairly versatile – you can add and substitute ingredients with greater freedom than you can with most other baked goods. To lower the fat content, substitute some of the oil with an equal amount of almost any fruit puree (applesauce, baby-food prunes, pumpkin puree, mashed bananas). You can also add nuts and dried fruits to your heart's content, and substitute one kind of nut, dried fruit or fresh fruit for another.

When you use dried fruit in a quick bread recipe, try soaking the fruit first. (Not only will this make the fruit itself moist and tender, but doing so will also preserve the moisture of the bread because the fruit will soak up less moisture from the batter while it bakes.) Simply place the dried fruit in a heatproof bowl and pour just enough boiling water to cover. Let it soak for 15 minutes or so, then drain and add to the finished batter. Alternatively, you can soak the fruit overnight in whiskey or rum for a more sophisticated taste. In either case, don't sprinkle dried fruit on top of the quick bread before baking - it will dry out and burn, making an unattractive (and tasteless) topper.

For a nice finishing touch – and a burst of flavor – try glazing your quick breads after they have cooled. Simply prepare a mixture of confectioners' sugar and a little milk, orange juice, or lemon juice and brush it over the top.

troubleshooting: quick breads

There are a few common problems that people encounter when baking quick breads. Luckily, most of these problems are easily avoidable once you understand the culprits:

- **The bread sticks to the pan**

  Unless you're using high-quality, nonstick metal or silicone baking pans, you should always grease the pans before you pour in the batter. Shortening works best, because its melting point is higher than any other kind of fat, providing a "shield" between the pan and the batter while the bread is baking. If you use a liquid fat – such as vegetable oil – it will simply be absorbed into the batter. People also experience sticking problems when they use low-fat bread recipes. The best solution to this problem is to more generously grease the pan, or invest in some really good nonstick pans. You can also prevent sticking by removing the bread from the pan within a few minutes of taking it out of the oven, before it has time to "set" in.

- **There are big holes and 'tunnels' in the bread, and/or the bread is tough**

  These problems are usually caused by overmixing. Combine the dry ingredients – flour, leavener, salt and spices – in one bowl and mix them thoroughly with a wire whisk. In another bowl, beat together the fat, sugar, and eggs in the order the recipe advises. Stir any other ingredients – fruit or fruit puree, nuts, flavorings – into the wet ingredients. Only when each bowl of ingredients is mixed thoroughly should they be combined. Pour the dry ingredients into the wet ones and fold them together gently by hand. Stir only until all the dry ingredients are moistened. Don't worry about a few lumps – they will disappear during baking.

- **There's a big crack down the middle of the quick bread loaf**

  Cracks occur when the top of the loaf "sets" in the heat of the oven before the bread is finished rising.

- **The bread looks done on the outside, but it's still raw in the middle**

  This is one of the most common quick bread problems, and it has several causes. First, your oven maybe too hot; try lowering the temperature and/or putting a loose tent of foil over the top of the bread so it won't burn before the middle has time to catch up. (FYI: Most ovens are inaccurate – usually off by 25 to 75 degrees F. The best way to get an accurate temperature is to use an oven thermometer that hangs from the oven rack.)

  Another factor in the "raw center" problem is using a different size pan than called for in the recipe. On the one hand, a nice thing about quick breads is the fact that you can use the same batter to make muffins, mini loaves, jumbo loaves, or just about any shape you want. On the other hand, each size requires slightly different baking times, and sometimes different baking temperatures, too. The larger and thicker the loaf, the longer it takes to bake. Be sure to adjust the baking time accordingly and check the bread often.

pies

Holiday pies are an important part of traditional holiday celebrations, and we have some great tips on how to get ahead of the game so there will be less to do on the big day.

Pie pastry can be made ahead of time and refrigerated for two to three days, or frozen for up to two weeks. Ready-made pie pastry may also be purchased in the refrigerated dough section of the supermarket. If you don't have a pie pan, frozen pie pastry may be purchased already in a disposable pan, which makes for easy cleanup.

When pre-baking a pie crust, fit the pastry into a pie pan, prick the bottom several times with a fork, and line it with aluminum foil or parchment paper. Fill it with pie weights, dried beans or rice. Bake at 425 degrees F (220 degrees C) until the edges begin to brown, about eight minutes. Remove the weights and paper or foil, and return it to the oven to bake until just lightly browned, three or four minutes. There is no reason to skimp on quality just because you are preparing in advance. You can make your own pumpkin or squash puree for fresh pies, divide it into recipe-size portions, and store it in the refrigerator for up to one week, or freeze for up to six months. Thaw in the refrigerator overnight, or in the microwave for immediate use.

Fresh sugar pumpkins are available starting in mid-October. These are the best choice for pumpkin pie. Simply cut the pumpkin in half, and remove the seeds and stringy bits. At this point, you can boil it, steam it, bake it (covered), or even cook it in the microwave. It is finished when the flesh can be pierced easily with a fork. Scoop the flesh out with a large spoon, leaving the skin behind. Puree the flesh in a blender or food processor, and use, refrigerate or freeze. This can also be done with any other winter squash.

For apple pies, you can purchase frozen sliced apples and use them while still frozen. Most pies will hold about two pounds of sliced apples. This saves the trouble of peeling and coring, and nobody will know the difference.

Cranberries are plentiful in the winter months, and are very convenient for freezing. Because of their low water content, fresh cranberries may be frozen in their package for up to one month. They also do not need to thaw before using.

cheesecake

It's one of the most luxurious desserts of all, but easy enough for anyone – even the novice baker – to attempt. Below are some pointers for making the best cheesecake possible.

Cracks are, by far, the most common woe among cheesecake bakers – these unsightly lines form in the middle of the cake during or after baking. To prevent the problem:

- **Bake the cheesecake in a water bath.** This keeps the oven-moisture high and the heat gentle – two important conditions for perfect cheesecake. To make a water bath, you set the cheesecake pan inside a roasting pan on the oven rack, then pour boiling water into the roasting pan until the water is at least halfway up the sides of the cheesecake pan, but NOT spilling over the top.

- **Don't overbake.** When cheesecake is perfectly done, there will still be a two-to-three-inch wobbly spot in the middle; the texture will firm up as the cake cools.
- **All cheesecakes shrink as they cool.** If you generously grease the sides of the pan before pouring in batter, the cake will be able to pull away from the pan rather than pulling apart from the middle.

Make your cheesecake look as spectacular as it tastes by dressing it up before serving. Try a fruity puree of fresh berries with a sprinkle of sugar or liqueur, or even chocolate curls created by microwaving a block of chocolate for a few seconds and scraping the softened edge with a potato peeler.

Cheesecakes freeze splendidly. For best results, transfer your cake to a cardboard circle and freeze unwrapped for a few hours. Once firm, thoroughly wrap in a double layer of plastic wrap, and then in heavy-duty foil. Use within a month. To thaw, simply place in the refrigerator overnight. Do not put any toppings or garnishes on the cake until ready to serve.

freezing cookies and cookie dough

Freezing cookies or cookie dough is a great way to plan ahead for holiday entertaining and gift-giving, or just to nice to have on hand anytime you want fresh, homemade cookies in a hurry. Before sticking them in the freezer, remember to label your dough and cookies with the variety and the date they were frozen.

Unbaked cookie dough: Dough can be kept frozen for 4 to 6 weeks. It will absorb any odd odors present in your freezer if it's not properly wrapped and sealed, so make sure to double-wrap it. Let the dough defrost in the refrigerator. This will take several hours, so plan ahead. The cookie doughs that freeze best are shortbreads, chocolate chip, peanut butter, refrigerator cookies, sugar cookies, and brownies. The types of cookie doughs that do not freeze well are cake-like cookies and cookies that have a very liquidy batter, such as madeleines and tuiles.

Baked cookies: Freezing baked cookies is a great way to preserve their freshness. Baked cookies will keep in the freezer for 3 or 4 weeks. Let the cookies cool completely, and then double-wrap them securely. When you are ready to eat your frozen cookies, just let them come to room temperature, or, for you impatient types, pop them in the microwave on high for about 30 seconds. We still haven't come across a baked cookie that doesn't freeze well, so feel free to freeze loads of assorted cookies to keep yourself supplied with homemade goodies, any time.

recipe tips

variations on a theme

You may wonder why we have more than one recipe for some items, such as sweet potatoes or stuffing. Don't worry – these are far from being duplicate recipes! Some dishes are so popular that our community members share multiple variations of them. In fact, when you visit Allrecipes.com, you'll find that we have dozens of variations on many of your favorite recipes. As we post new versions of a recipe, we'll add a Roman numeral to the title to distinguish it (for example, the "Pumpkin Bread IV" recipe which appears in this book). There are lots of different ways to approach even the old standards, and in this book you can enjoy your next batch of stuffing with juicy sausage and dried cranberries, with cornbread and sweet apples, or with the classic celery and onions. Come see us at Allrecipes.com to explore new renditions of all your old favorites.

about the recipes

Half the fun of an Allrecipes recipe is the story behind it – each of our recipes has comments submitted by the contributor to help explain how the recipe came about, what it's like, or how they use it. As the editors of the Allrecipes cookbooks, both online and in print, the staff works hard to preserve the character of the contributed recipe, but also strives to ensure consistency, accuracy, and completeness in the published version and throughout the collection.

all in the timing

At the top right corner of every recipe in the book, you'll find "Preparation," "Cooking," and "Ready In" times. These times are approximate. Depending on how fast you chop vegetables, how practiced you are at trussing a turkey, whether or not you have a dozen relatives underfoot, and any number of other factors – you may find that it takes less or more time than what we've estimated. The "Ready In" times will tell you, on average, how much time the recipe takes from start to finish. With a few recipes, this will be slightly longer than the "Preparation" time plus the "Cooking" time. These are recipes that contain intermediate steps that aren't prepping or cooking, such as waiting for the meat to marinate or the dough to rise. Refer to the "Ready In" time to know roughly how long you need between opening the book and serving the finished dish.

need help? we're here for you!

Need more information about an unfamiliar ingredient or cooking term, general cooking information, or difficult technique? We've got a whole section of Allrecipes.com dedicated to giving you all the help you need. In our "Cooking Basics" section, you can search for thousands of kitchen terms, follow photo-filled step-by-step tutorials to learn important cooking skills, and browse or search hundreds of articles that will help you decide what to make and teach you how to make it. You can access the "Cooking Basics" section at Allrecipes:
http://allrecipes.com/cb/

beyond the book

Each of the recipes in this book can be accessed online at Allrecipes.com. The online versions have some handy, whiz-bang features we didn't manage to squeeze into this book. If you'd like to adjust the number of servings for a recipe, view detailed nutritional information, convert the measurements to metric, or email a copy to a friend, it's all just a click away! The online version also includes user reviews that often come with variations and handy tips. We've created a special place on Allrecipes.com where you can find any recipe in this book simply by entering its page number. Check it out!
http://allrecipes.com/tnt/thanksxmas/page.asp

your two cents

Once you try a recipe in this book, you can tell the rest of the world all about it. First, locate the recipe on Allrecipes.com (see above). Next, click on the link that says "Add to Recipe Box" (below the recipe's description). Then, follow the instructions to set up a FREE recipe box of your own. Once you've added the recipe to your box, you can rate it on a scale of 1 to 5 stars and share your comments with the millions of other people who use the site. Come tell us what you think!

tried and true

If you'd like to find out more about this book, the recipes, and other Allrecipes "tried & true" cookbooks - join us online at **http://allrecipes.com/tnt/** or send us an email at **tnt@allrecipes.com**

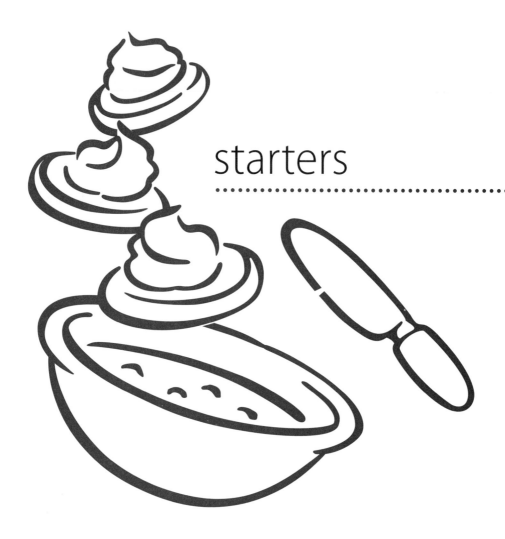

starters

Some of the best holiday memories are made while waiting for the last few guests to arrive – as the food is still simmering and the roast is resting. Everyone can appreciate sipping on a fragrant spiced cider while chatting over a savory baked dip or cheese ball. This chapter contains famously easy and tasty snacks to entertain your guests while they wait for the feast to begin.

Artichoke and Roasted Red Pepper Dip

Submitted by: **Eileen**

Makes: 3 cups

Preparation: 10 minutes

Cooking: 40 minutes

Ready In: 50 minutes

"A hot tasty dip that is sure to please everyone. Artichoke hearts and roasted red peppers add a pleasant zing to this mild crowd pleaser that's perfect for crackers or bread."

INGREDIENTS

2 tablespoons butter

1 leek, diced

2 (6.5 ounce) jars marinated artichoke hearts, drained and chopped

1 (7 ounce) jar roasted red peppers, drained and chopped

3/4 cup freshly grated Parmesan cheese

3 tablespoons mayonnaise

DIRECTIONS

1. Preheat oven to 350°F (175°C).

2. Melt butter in a saucepan over medium heat. Saute diced leek until tender. Stir in the artichoke hearts, roasted red peppers, Parmesan cheese, and mayonnaise. Transfer to an 8x8 inch baking dish.

3. Bake for 30 minutes in the preheated oven, or until bubbly and lightly browned.

Luscious Spinach Artichoke Dip

Submitted by: **Youri**

Makes: 3 cups
Preparation: 10 minutes
Cooking: 25 minutes
Ready In: 35 minutes

"This is a rich, delicious dip that can be served with tortilla chips or slices of toasted French bread. It can be easily substituted with fat-free ingredients for all of you health freaks out there! It's an absolute hit at all parties. Here are a few suggested garnishes: shredded Monterey Jack cheese, chopped red bell peppers, parsley, sliced mushrooms, or bread crumbs."

INGREDIENTS

1 (14 ounce) can artichoke hearts, drained and chopped

1/2 (10 ounce) package frozen chopped spinach, thawed

1/2 cup sour cream

1/4 cup mayonnaise

1/4 cup cream cheese

1/4 cup grated Romano cheese

1/4 teaspoon minced garlic

DIRECTIONS

1. Preheat oven to 375°F (190°C).

2. In a small baking dish, mix together artichoke hearts, spinach, sour cream, mayonnaise, cream cheese, Romano cheese, and garlic. Cover dish.

3. Bake until heated through and bubbly, about 25 minutes.

Pumpkin Dip

Submitted by: **Sue Case**

Makes: 4 cups

Preparation: 15 minutes

Ready In: 15 minutes

"An excellent appetizer for the holidays! Serve with ginger snaps. MMMMM!"

INGREDIENTS

1 (8 ounce) package cream cheese, softened

2 cups confectioners' sugar

1 (15 ounce) can solid pack pumpkin

1 tablespoon ground cinnamon

1 tablespoon pumpkin pie spice

1 teaspoon frozen orange juice concentrate

DIRECTIONS

1. In a medium bowl, blend cream cheese and confectioners' sugar until smooth. Gradually mix in the pumpkin. Stir in the cinnamon, pumpkin pie spice, and orange juice until smooth and well blended. Chill until serving.

Blueberry Brie

Submitted by: **Dana Cole**

Makes: 32 servings

Preparation: 5 minutes

Cooking: 15 minutes

Ready In: 20 minutes

"Warm Blueberry Brie...we have this every year at our work's Christmas party. It is so tasty, it's addictive! You can also make this with raspberry sauce or sun dried tomatoes, both of which taste excellent. This will cook in the microwave in about 3 minutes. Serve with warm French baguette slices!"

INGREDIENTS

1 (2.2 pound) wheel Brie cheese

1 (16 ounce) can blueberry pie filling

DIRECTIONS

1. Preheat oven to 350°F (175°C).

2. Place Brie cheese in a baking dish. Pour blueberry pie filling over the top.

3. Bake until hot, about 10 to 15 minutes.

Chutney Baked Brie

Submitted by: **Hillary Quinn**

Makes: 32 servings

Preparation: 10 minutes

Cooking: 15 minutes

Ready In: 25 minutes

"This round wheel of Brie is dusted with curry powder, then spread with a mango chutney, studded with chopped cashews, and baked until the cheese inside the rind is melted. The sweet/savory combination is creamy and delicious."

INGREDIENTS

1 (2.2 pound) wheel Brie cheese

2 teaspoons ground curry powder

1 (12 ounce) jar mango chutney

1 cup chopped cashews

1 French baguette, cut into ¹/₂ inch slices

DIRECTIONS

1. Preheat oven to 350°F (175°C).

2. Sprinkle curry powder over top and sides of Brie; rub the curry powder into the rind to thoroughly coat the surface. Place the Brie wheel in a large pie plate or oven proof dish. Spread a generous layer of chutney over the top, and evenly sprinkle with cashews.

3. Bake 15 minutes in the preheated oven, or until cashews are slightly golden and cheese inside the rind is melted. Serve with slices of baguette.

Bread Pot Fondue

Submitted by: **Laurie**

Makes: 32 servings

Preparation: 20 minutes

Cooking: 1 hour 10 minutes

Ready In: 1 hour 30 minutes

"This is a yummy appetizer. Creamy, cheesy and spicy - a variety of flavors are blended throughout. A real treat for your palate. Easy to put together, and well worth the time in the oven. You can bake the scooped out pieces of bread and use them for dipping. I usually buy an extra loaf of bread, just for dipping."

INGREDIENTS

1 (1 pound) loaf round bread

1 (8 ounce) package shredded Cheddar cheese

2 (3 ounce) packages cream cheese

1½ cups sour cream

1 cup cooked ham, diced

½ cup chopped green onions

1 (4 ounce) can diced green chile peppers

1 teaspoon Worcestershire sauce

2 tablespoons vegetable oil

1 tablespoon butter, melted

DIRECTIONS

1. Preheat oven to 350°F (175°C). Cut a circle in the top of the bread. Remove top, and set aside. Hollow out the loaf, reserving removed bread for dipping.

2. In a medium bowl, mix the Cheddar cheese, cream cheese, sour cream, ham, green onions, green chile peppers, and Worcestershire sauce. Spoon into the bread bowl, and replace the top. Wrap loaf tightly in foil, and place on a baking sheet.

3. Bake until cheese is melted and bubbly, about 1 hour.

4. Meanwhile, cut reserved bread into small pieces. Toss with oil and melted butter, and place on the baking sheet. Toast in oven until golden brown, about 10 to 15 minutes.

Cheese Ball

Submitted by: **Ellen Rainey**

Makes: 1 large cheese ball

Preparation: 15 minutes

Ready In: 2 hours 15 minutes

"This is a wonderful cheese ball. It is very easy to make and simply delicious. Whenever I make it for gatherings or work it always gets great reviews. Serve with an assortment of crackers."

INGREDIENTS

2 (8 ounce) packages cream cheese, softened

3 1/2 cups shredded sharp Cheddar cheese

1 (1 ounce) package Ranch-style dressing mix

2 cups chopped pecans

4 pecan halves

DIRECTIONS

1. In a large bowl, mix together cream cheese, Cheddar cheese, and dressing mix. Form into one large ball or two smaller balls. Roll in chopped pecans to coat surface. Decorate the top with pecan halves. Refrigerate for at least 2 hours, or overnight.

Hot Pepper Jelly

Submitted by: **Wendy Furbay**

Makes: 6 (8 ounce) jars

Preparation: 30 minutes

Cooking: 15 minutes

Ready In: 1 hour 45 minutes

"Enjoy this spicy treat on crackers with cream cheese. It also makes a festive holiday appetizer."

INGREDIENTS

2¹/₂ cups finely chopped red bell peppers

1¹/₄ cups finely chopped green bell peppers

¹/₄ cup finely chopped jalapeno peppers

1 cup apple cider vinegar

1 (1.75 ounce) package powdered pectin

5 cups white sugar

DIRECTIONS

1. Sterilize 6 (8 ounce) canning jars and lids according to manufacturer's instructions. Heat water in a hot water canner.

2. Place red bell peppers, green bell peppers, and jalapeno peppers in a large saucepan over high heat. Mix in vinegar and fruit pectin. Stirring constantly, bring mixture to a full rolling boil. Quickly stir in sugar. Return to full rolling boil, and boil exactly 1 minute, stirring constantly. Remove from heat, and skim off any foam.

3. Quickly ladle jelly into sterile jars, filling to within ¼ inch of the tops. Cover with flat lids, and screw on bands tightly.

4. Place jars in rack, and slowly lower jars into canner. The water should cover the jars completely, and should be hot, but not boiling. Bring water to a boil, and process for 5 minutes.

Feta Cheese Foldovers

Submitted by: **Chris Lipo**

Makes: 12 servings

Preparation: 20 minutes

Cooking: 20 minutes

Ready In: 40 minutes

"Golden puffed pastries are filled with a feta cheese mixture. These can be made ahead, and popped into the oven after your guests arrive."

INGREDIENTS

8 ounces feta cheese, crumbled

3 tablespoons finely chopped green onions

1 egg, beaten

1 (17.5 ounce) package frozen puff pastry, thawed

1 egg yolk, beaten with 1 teaspoon water

DIRECTIONS

1. Preheat oven to 375 °F (190°C).

2. In a small bowl, blend feta cheese, green onions, and egg. Cut pastry into 12 (3 inch) squares. Place a mounded tablespoon of feta mixture in the center of each square. Moisten edges with water, and fold pastry over filling to form a triangle. Press edges together firmly with a fork to seal. Lightly brush pastries with the egg yolk mixture.

3. Bake for 20 minutes in the preheated oven, or until golden brown. Serve warm or at room temperature.

Rockin' Oysters Rockefeller

Submitted by: **Cassandra Kennedy**

Makes: 16 servings

Preparation: 30 minutes

Cooking: 30 minutes

Ready In: 1 hour

"This is a slight variation on the classic dish Oysters Rockefeller. Serve this delicious dish and watch your guests cry, 'I love you!!!'"

INGREDIENTS

48 fresh, unopened oysters

1 1/2 cups beer

2 cloves garlic

seasoned salt to taste

7 black peppercorns

1/2 cup butter

1 onion, chopped

1 clove garlic, crushed

1 (10 ounce) package frozen chopped spinach, thawed and drained

8 ounces Monterey Jack cheese, shredded

8 ounces fontina cheese, shredded

8 ounces mozzarella cheese, shredded

1/2 cup milk

2 teaspoons salt, or to taste

1 teaspoon ground black pepper

2 tablespoons fine bread crumbs

DIRECTIONS

1. Clean oysters, and place in a large stockpot. Pour in beer and enough water to cover oysters; add 2 cloves garlic, seasoned salt, and peppercorns. Bring to a boil. Remove from heat, drain, and cool.

2. Once oysters are cooled, break off and discard the top shell. Arrange the oysters on a baking sheet. Preheat oven to 425°F (220°C.)

3. Melt butter in a saucepan over medium heat. Cook onion and garlic in butter until soft. Reduce heat to low, and stir in spinach, Monterey Jack, fontina, and mozzarella. Cook until cheese melts, stirring frequently. Stir in the milk, and season with salt and pepper. Spoon sauce over each oyster, just filling the shell. Sprinkle with bread crumbs.

4. Bake until golden and bubbly, approximately 8 to 10 minutes.

Stuffed Mushrooms IV

Submitted by: **Jennifer**

Makes: 12 servings

Preparation: 20 minutes

Cooking: 40 minutes

Ready In: 1 hour

"An 18th Century recipe that I have altered slightly. Better make a double batch because these go fast. Sausage can be substituted for ground beef if you'd like."

INGREDIENTS

12 fresh mushrooms

¹/₂ pound ground beef

1 tablespoon minced onion

1 clove garlic, minced

1 tablespoon butter

¹/₄ cup bread crumbs

salt and pepper to taste

¹/₄ cup heavy cream

¹/₄ cup butter, melted

1 teaspoon chili powder

DIRECTIONS

1. Preheat oven to 425°F (220°C). Remove and chop mushroom stems.

2. In a saucepan over medium heat, combine ground beef, onion, and garlic. Cook until beef is no longer pink; drain. Mix in chopped mushroom stems, 1 tablespoon butter, bread crumbs, salt, and pepper. Cook, stirring frequently, for 5 minutes. Remove from heat, and stir in cream.

3. Dip mushroom caps in ¼ cup melted butter, and stuff generously with meat mixture. Arrange stuffed mushrooms in a baking dish. Sprinkle with chili powder.

4. Bake for 20 to 25 minutes in the preheated oven.

Cocktail Meatballs

Submitted by: **Lara**

Makes: 10 servings

Preparation: 20 minutes

Cooking: 1 hour 25 minutes

Ready In: 1 hour 45 minutes

"These tasty meatballs will disappear quickly from anyone's holiday party. My mom makes them every year for New Year's Eve, and now so do I. These do very well in a slow cooker, as you can simmer them before serving, as well as keep them hot for the duration of your party."

INGREDIENTS

1 pound lean ground beef

1 egg

2 tablespoons water

1/2 cup bread crumbs

3 tablespoons minced onion

1 (8 ounce) can jellied cranberry sauce

3/4 cup chili sauce

1 tablespoon brown sugar

1 1/2 teaspoons lemon juice

DIRECTIONS

1. Preheat oven to 350°F (175°C).

2. In a large bowl, mix together the ground beef, egg, water, bread crumbs, and minced onion. Roll into small meatballs.

3. Bake in preheated oven for 20 to 25 minutes, turning once.

4. In a slow cooker or large saucepan over low heat, blend the cranberry sauce, chili sauce, brown sugar, and lemon juice. Add meatballs, and simmer for 1 hour before serving.

Ranch Oyster Crackers

Submitted by: **Jackie Smith**

Makes: 5 cups

Preparation: 10 minutes

Cooking: 20 minutes

Ready In: 30 minutes

"These seasoned oyster crackers make an easy snack for any party occasion."

INGREDIENTS

1 (1 ounce) package Ranch-style dressing mix

¹/₂ teaspoon dried dill weed

¹/₄ cup vegetable oil

¹/₄ teaspoon lemon pepper (optional)

¹/₄ teaspoon garlic powder (optional)

5 cups oyster crackers

DIRECTIONS

1. Preheat oven to 250°F (120°C).

2. In a large bowl, combine the dressing mix, dill weed, vegetable oil, lemon pepper, and garlic powder. Add oyster crackers, and toss to coat. Spread evenly on a baking sheet.

3. Bake for 15 to 20 minutes in the preheated oven, stirring gently after 10 minutes. Remove from oven, and allow to cool before serving.

Candy Cane Cocoa

Submitted by: **Verushka**

Makes: 4 (1 cup) servings

Preparation: 5 minutes

Cooking: 10 minutes

Ready In: 15 minutes

"The rich flavor of chocolate combines so well with peppermint. This is the perfect drink to sip while trimming the tree."

INGREDIENTS

4 cups milk

3 (1 ounce) squares semisweet chocolate, chopped

4 peppermint candy canes, crushed

1 cup whipped cream

4 small peppermint candy canes

DIRECTIONS

1. In a saucepan, heat milk until hot, but not boiling. Whisk in the chocolate and the crushed peppermint candies until melted and smooth. Pour hot cocoa into four mugs, and garnish with whipped cream. Serve each with a candy cane stirring stick.

Luscious Eggnog

Submitted by: **Carolyn**

Makes: 10 (4 ounce) servings

Preparation: 15 minutes

Cooking: 15 minutes

Ready In: 1 hour 30 minutes

"When serving, keep the bowl of eggnog resting in a bowl of ice to keep it well chilled!"

INGREDIENTS

3 eggs, lightly beaten

1/3 cup white sugar

salt to taste

2 1/2 cups milk

1 teaspoon vanilla extract

1 cup heavy cream

2 tablespoons confectioners' sugar

1/2 teaspoon vanilla extract

1/2 cup rum (optional)

2 drops yellow food coloring

1 pinch ground nutmeg

DIRECTIONS

1. In a heavy, saucepan, combine eggs, white sugar, and salt; gradually stir in milk. Stirring constantly, cook for 10 to 15 minutes over medium heat, until mixture just coats a metal spoon. Remove from heat, and stir in 1 teaspoon vanilla extract. Place saucepan over ice water until custard cools, and then refrigerate until chilled.

2. In a chilled bowl, combine heavy cream, confectioners' sugar, and 1/2 teaspoon vanilla extract. Beat until stiff peaks form. Stir in rum and yellow food coloring. Fold whipped cream mixture into the cooled custard. Pour into serving bowl, and sprinkle with nutmeg. Serve immediately.

Hot Buttered Rum Batter

Submitted by: **Sheri Marr**

Makes: 100 servings

Preparation: 10 minutes

"This is THE batter to use for absolutely delicious and buttery Hot Buttered Rums! You can keep this in the freezer for up to 3 months."

INGREDIENTS

1 pound butter

1 pound brown sugar

1 pound confectioners' sugar

1 quart vanilla ice cream, softened

1 tablespoon ground cinnamon

1 teaspoon ground nutmeg

DIRECTIONS

1. Melt butter in a large pot over medium heat. Blend in brown sugar and confectioners' sugar. Remove from heat, and whisk in the ice cream, cinnamon, and nutmeg. Pour mixture into a plastic container, seal, and freeze.

2. In a coffee mug, measure 1 tablespoon Hot Buttered Rum Batter and 1 fluid ounce of rum, then fill cup with boiling water. Stir, and sprinkle top of drink with nutmeg.

Original Irish Cream

Submitted by: **Mom**

Makes: 4 cups

Preparation: 15 minutes

Ready In: 15 minutes

"Irish whiskey mixed with cream and sugar with hints of coffee, chocolate, vanilla, and almond. Will keep for 2 months if refrigerated."

INGREDIENTS

1 cup heavy cream

1 (14 ounce) can sweetened condensed milk

1 2/3 cups Irish whiskey

1 teaspoon instant coffee granules

2 tablespoons chocolate syrup

1 teaspoon vanilla extract

1 teaspoon almond extract

DIRECTIONS

1. In a blender, combine heavy cream, sweetened condensed milk, Irish whiskey, instant coffee, chocolate syrup, vanilla extract, and almond extract. Blend on high for 20 to 30 seconds. Store in a tightly sealed container in the refrigerator. Shake well before serving.

Coffee Liqueur

Submitted by: **Cathie**

Makes: 8 cups

Preparation: 15 minutes

Cooking: 10 minutes

Ready In: 1 hour

"This is an easy recipe for making a coffee flavored liqueur. This can be used in any recipe that calls for coffee flavored liqueur, as a cordial alone, mixed with milk or more vodka, etc."

INGREDIENTS

4 cups white sugar

4 cups water

3/4 cup instant coffee granules

2 tablespoons vanilla extract

4 cups vodka

DIRECTIONS

1. In a 3 quart saucepan over medium heat, combine the sugar and water. Bring to a boil, reduce heat, and simmer for 10 minutes. Remove from heat, stir in instant coffee, and allow to cool.

2. When cool, stir in vanilla extract and vodka. Pour into clean bottles. Close bottles tightly, and store in a cool dark place.

Warm and Spicy Autumn Punch

Submitted by: **Michele O'Sullivan**

Makes: 16 (4 ounce) servings

Preparation: 20 minutes

Cooking: 40 minutes

Ready In: 1 hour

"The aroma of this punch tells you that fall is in the air. Make a batch, and your home will have a fragrance that will alert anyone's sense of smell."

INGREDIENTS

2 oranges

8 whole cloves

6 cups apple juice

1 cinnamon stick

1/4 teaspoon ground nutmeg

1/4 cup honey

3 tablespoons lemon juice

2 1/4 cups pineapple juice

DIRECTIONS

1. Preheat oven to 350°F (175°C). Stud the whole oranges with cloves, and bake for 30 minutes.

2. In a large saucepan, combine the apple juice and cinnamon stick. Bring to a boil, reduce heat to medium, and simmer 5 minutes. Remove from heat, and stir in the nutmeg, honey, lemon juice, and pineapple juice.

3. Serve hot in a punch bowl with the 2 clove-studded baked oranges floating on top.

Hot Spiced Cider

Submitted by: **Sara**

Makes: 2 quarts

Preparation: 5 minutes

Cooking: 5 minutes

Ready In: 10 minutes

"This recipe uses an automatic coffee maker to brew the cider. If you don't own one, heat it in a slow cooker or a saucepan over medium heat on the stovetop. Grab your mugs and dive into this hot drink! Clean your coffee maker according to the manufacturer's instructions before using for coffee again."

INGREDIENTS

1/4 cup packed brown sugar

1/2 teaspoon whole allspice

1 teaspoon whole cloves

1 cinnamon stick

1/4 teaspoon salt

1 pinch ground nutmeg

1 large orange, quartered with peel

2 quarts apple cider

DIRECTIONS

1. Place filter in coffee basket, and fill with brown sugar, allspice, cloves, cinnamon stick, salt, nutmeg, and orange wedges. Pour apple cider into coffee pot where the water usually goes. Brew, and serve hot.

Gluehwein

Submitted by: **Else**

Makes: 6 (4 ounce) servings

Preparation: 10 minutes

Cooking: 35 minutes

Ready In: 45 minutes

"Gluehwein is a German/Austrian winter-holiday drink that most tourists know as an after-ski drink. After you come in out of the snow, it is supposed to make you glow with warmth again. Watch it: Since you drink this wine warm, the alcohol goes to your head extra quick! Drink when you really have come in, and do not have to go out again! This is the one my father used to make for New Year's Eve."

INGREDIENTS

³/₄ cup water

³/₄ cup white sugar

1 cinnamon stick

1 orange

10 whole cloves

1 (750 milliliter) bottle red wine

DIRECTIONS

1. In a saucepan, combine the water, sugar, and cinnamon stick. Bring to a boil, reduce heat, and simmer.

2. Cut the orange in half, and squeeze the juice into the simmering water. Push the cloves into the outside of the orange peel, and place peel in the simmering water. Continue simmering for 30 minutes, until thick and syrupy.

3. Pour in the wine, and heat until steaming but not simmering. Remove the clove-studded orange halves. Serve hot in mugs or glasses that have been preheated in warm water (cold glasses will break).

Christmas Punch

Submitted by: **LV**

Makes: 20 (4 ounce) servings

Preparation: 15 minutes

Ready In: 2 hours 15 minutes

"Delicious punch! Great for holidays, showers, parties! Make extra!"

INGREDIENTS

1/2 cup white sugar

2 cups orange juice

2/3 cup lemon juice

1 (4 ounce) jar maraschino cherries, with juice

1 fluid ounce triple sec liqueur

1 (750 milliliter) bottle light rum

1 orange, sliced into rounds

1 lemon, sliced into rounds

1 (8 ounce) can pineapple chunks

1 liter carbonated water

ice

DIRECTIONS

1. In a punch bowl, combine sugar, orange juice, and lemon juice. Stir until sugar dissolves. Add cherries, triple sec, light rum, orange slices, lemon slices, and pineapple chunks. Refrigerate for 1 to 2 hours to allow flavors to blend.

2. Pour in carbonated water, and add ice just before serving.

Holiday Punch

Submitted by: **Erin Paynter**

Makes: 40 (4 ounce) servings

Preparation: 10 minutes

Ready In: 2 hours 10 minutes

"Good for when friends drop by during the holidays. Quick and tasty. Add rum for a bit of a kick."

INGREDIENTS

4 cups cranberry juice cocktail

8 cups prepared lemonade

2 cups orange juice

1 (4 ounce) jar maraschino cherries

1 (2 liter) bottle ginger ale

1 orange, sliced in rounds

DIRECTIONS

1. In a large punch bowl, combine cranberry juice cocktail, lemonade, and orange juice. Stir in the maraschino cherries. Refrigerate for 2 hours or more.

2. When ready to serve, pour in the ginger ale. Garnish each glass with an orange slice.

Luscious Slush Punch

Submitted by: **Valerie**

Makes: 50 (4 ounce) servings

Preparation: 15 minutes

Cooking: 5 minutes

Ready In: 8 hours 20 minutes

"This is without a doubt the best punch I've ever had! Makes enough for 2 punch bowls. This is our Christmas Eve punch tradition, and there is never a drop left!"

INGREDIENTS

2¹/₂ cups white sugar

6 cups water

2 (3 ounce) packages strawberry flavored gelatin mix

1 (46 fluid ounce) can pineapple juice

²/₃ cup lemon juice

1 quart orange juice

2 (2 liter) bottles lemon-lime flavored carbonated beverage

DIRECTIONS

1. In a large saucepan, combine sugar, water, and strawberry flavored gelatin. Boil for 3 minutes. Stir in pineapple juice, lemon juice, and orange juice. Divide mixture in half, and freeze in 2 separate containers.

2. When ready to serve, place the frozen contents of one container in a punch bowl, and stir in 1 bottle of lemon-lime soda until slushy.

main dishes

Whether your holiday centerpiece is a glistening glazed ham, a robust and juicy prime rib, or the traditional turkey roasted to crispy, golden perfection, there is a recipe in this chapter that is sure to satisfy. Imagine the gasps of delight as you proudly serve up one of these succulent superstars.

Easy Herb Roasted Turkey

Submitted by: **Lisa Hamm**

Makes: 1 (12 pound) turkey

Preparation: 15 minutes

Cooking: 3 hours 30 minutes

Ready In: 4 hours 15 minutes

"This is an easy and delicious recipe for a turkey that is perfectly browned on the outside while being both tender and juicy on the inside!"

INGREDIENTS

1 (12 pound) whole turkey

3/4 cup olive oil

2 tablespoons garlic powder

2 teaspoons dried basil

1 teaspoon ground sage

1 teaspoon salt

1/2 teaspoon black pepper

2 cups water

DIRECTIONS

1. Preheat oven to 325°F (165°C). Clean turkey (discard giblets and organs), and place in a roasting pan with a lid.

2. In a small bowl, combine olive oil, garlic powder, dried basil, ground sage, salt, and black pepper. Using a basting brush, apply the mixture to the outside of the uncooked turkey. Pour water into the bottom of the roasting pan, and cover.

3. Bake for 3 to 3½ hours, or until the internal temperature of the thickest part of the thigh measures 180°F (80°C). Remove bird from oven, and allow to stand for about 30 minutes before carving.

Rosemary Roasted Turkey

Submitted by: **Star Pooley**

Makes: 1 (12 pound) turkey

Preparation: 25 minutes

Cooking: 4 hours

Ready In: 4 hours 45 minutes

"This recipe makes your turkey moist and full of flavor. You can also use this recipe for Cornish game hens, chicken breasts or roasting chicken. Select a turkey sized according to the amount of people you will be serving."

INGREDIENTS

3/4 cup olive oil

3 tablespoons minced garlic

2 tablespoons chopped fresh rosemary

1 tablespoon chopped fresh basil

1 tablespoon Italian seasoning

1 teaspoon ground black pepper

salt to taste

1 (12 pound) whole turkey

DIRECTIONS

1. Preheat oven to 325°F (165°C).

2. In a small bowl, mix the olive oil, garlic, rosemary, basil, Italian seasoning, black pepper and salt. Set aside.

3. Wash the turkey inside and out; pat dry. Remove any large fat deposits. Loosen the skin from the breast. This is done by slowly working your fingers between the breast and the skin. Work it loose to the end of the drumstick, being careful not to tear the skin.

4. Using your hand, spread a generous amount of the rosemary mixture under the breast skin and down the thigh and leg. Rub the remainder of the rosemary mixture over the outside of the breast. Use toothpicks to seal skin over any exposed breast meat.

5. Place the turkey on a rack in a roasting pan. Add about ¼ inch of water to the bottom of the pan. Roast in the preheated oven 3 to 4 hours, or until the internal temperature of the bird reaches 180°F (80°C).

The World's Best Turkey

Submitted by: **Sarah**

"This recipe makes a deliciously moist turkey."

Makes: 1 (12 pound) turkey

Preparation: 20 minutes

Cooking: 3 hours 30 minutes

Ready In: 4 hours 10 minutes

INGREDIENTS

1 (12 pound) whole turkey, neck and giblets removed

1/2 cup butter, cubed

2 apples, cored and halved

1 tablespoon garlic powder

salt and pepper to taste

2/3 (750 milliliter) bottle champagne

DIRECTIONS

1. Preheat oven to 350°F (175°C).

2. Rinse turkey, and pat dry. Gently loosen turkey breast skin, and insert pieces of butter between the skin and breast. Place apples inside the turkey's cavity. Sprinkle with garlic powder, salt, and pepper. Place turkey in a roasting bag, and pour champagne over the inside and outside of the bird. Close bag, and place turkey in a roasting pan.

3. Bake turkey 3 to 3½ hours in the preheated oven, or until the internal temperature is 180°F (80°C) when measured in the meatiest part of the thigh. Remove turkey from bag, and let stand for at least 20 minutes before carving.

Homestyle Turkey, the Michigander Way

Submitted by: **Robin C.**

Makes: 1 (12 pound) turkey

Preparation: 10 minutes

Cooking: 5 hours

Ready In: 5 hours 10 minutes

"A simple, down to basics recipe when it comes to the good old tom turkey."

INGREDIENTS

1 (12 pound) whole turkey

6 tablespoons butter, divided

4 cups warm water

3 tablespoons chicken bouillon

2 tablespoons dried parsley

2 tablespoons dried minced onion

2 tablespoons seasoning salt

DIRECTIONS

1. Preheat oven to 350°F (175°C). Rinse and wash turkey. Discard the giblets, or add to pan if they are anyone's favorites.

2. Place turkey in a Dutch oven or roasting pan. Separate the skin over the breast to make little pockets. Put 3 tablespoons of the butter on both sides between the skin and breast meat. This makes for very juicy breast meat.

3. In a medium bowl, combine the water with the bouillon. Sprinkle in the parsley and minced onion. Pour over the top of the turkey. Sprinkle seasoning salt over the turkey.

4. Cover with foil, and bake in the preheated oven 3½ to 4 hours, until the internal temperature of the turkey reaches 180°F (80°C). For the last 45 minutes or so, remove the foil so the turkey will brown nicely.

Awesome Tangerine-Glazed Turkey

Submitted by: **Stacy M. Polcyn**

Makes: 1 (10 pound) turkey

Preparation: 45 minutes

Cooking: 3 hours 30 minutes

Ready In: 4 hours 15 minutes

"I guarantee that you will receive rave reviews on Thanksgiving Day with this recipe! Garnish with fresh thyme, rosemary, and bay leaf. The turkey is stuffed with Awesome Sausage Apple and Dried Cranberry Stuffing."

INGREDIENTS

3/4 cup unsalted butter, divided

3/4 cup canola oil

1 1/2 cups tangerine juice

1 (10 pound) whole turkey, neck and giblets reserved

2 1/4 cups Awesome Sausage, Apple and Cranberry Stuffing

salt and pepper to taste

2 1/4 cups turkey stock

3 tablespoons all-purpose flour

DIRECTIONS

1. Melt 6 tablespoons butter with canola oil and tangerine juice in a saucepan over medium heat. Remove from heat, and allow to cool about 5 minutes. Soak a piece of cheesecloth large enough to drape over the turkey in the mixture.

2. Preheat oven to 425°F (220°C). Clean turkey, and season body cavity with salt and pepper. Loosely pack the neck cavity and body cavity with stuffing. Tie drumsticks together, spread 6 tablespoons butter over the turkey, and season with salt and pepper. Place turkey in a shallow roasting pan.

3. Roast turkey for 25 minutes in the preheated oven, and then arrange soaked cheesecloth over turkey. Reduce oven temperature to 325°F (110°C). Continue roasting 1 hour. Leaving the cheesecloth draped over the turkey, baste with the tangerine juice mixture. Continue roasting about 2 hours, basting occasionally, until the internal temperature of the thickest part of the thigh reaches 180°F (80°C) and the stuffing inside the body cavity reaches 165°F (70°C). Discard cheesecloth, and place turkey on a serving platter. Allow turkey to cool about 25 minutes before carving.

4. Skim fat from pan juices, and reserve 1/4 cup fat and skimmed pan juices. In the baking pan, mix pan juices with 1 cup turkey stock; cook over high heat, stirring to scrape the bottom of the pan.

5. In a saucepan over low heat, whisk together reserved 1/4 cup fat and flour until thickened, about 3 minutes. Stir in pan juices and remaining turkey stock, and add neck and giblets. Simmer 10 minutes, stirring constantly, until giblets are cooked through. Strain through a sieve, and serve with the turkey and stuffing.

Deep-Fried Turkey

Submitted by: **Tim and Meredith**

Makes: 1 (12 pound) turkey

Preparation: 30 minutes

Cooking: 45 minutes

Ready In: 1 hour 30 minutes

"This is an awesome Cajun recipe. Deep-frying makes the turkey crispy on the outside and super juicy on the inside (even the white meat). It also leaves the heat outside! You can deep-fry the turkey in either peanut or vegetable oil, your choice. We use a 26 quart aluminum pot with a drain basket."

INGREDIENTS

3 gallons peanut oil for frying, or as needed

1 (12 pound) whole turkey, neck and giblets removed

$1/4$ cup Creole seasoning

1 white onion

DIRECTIONS

1. In a large stockpot or turkey fryer, heat oil to 400°F (200°C). Be sure to leave room for the turkey, or the oil will spill over. Layer a large platter with food-safe paper bags.

2. Rinse turkey, and thoroughly pat dry with paper towels. Rub Creole seasoning over turkey inside and out. Make sure the hole at the neck is open at least 2 inches so the oil can flow freely through the bird.

3. Place the whole onion and turkey in drain basket. The turkey should be placed in basket neck end first. Slowly lower basket into hot oil to completely cover turkey. Maintain the temperature of the oil at 350°F (175°C), and cook turkey for 3½ minutes per pound, about 45 minutes.

4. Carefully remove basket from oil, and drain turkey. Insert a meat thermometer into the thickest part of the thigh; the internal temperature must be 180°F (80°C). Finish draining turkey on the prepared platter.

Editorial Note: See our Fried Turkey tips, page 33.

Turkey in a Smoker

Submitted by: **Doug Kacsir**

Makes: 1 (10 pound) turkey

Preparation: 20 minutes

Cooking: 10 hours

Ready In: 10 hours 20 minutes

"This is a great recipe for smoked turkey. A barbecue grill is nearly impossible to cook a large bird. A smoker is best for this. I prefer hickory chips or hickory wood. Hickory generates a more even smokiness than other woods, and it does not matter whether the wood is green or seasoned. Mesquite, if not well seasoned, will generate a creosote type coating because of the sap that oozes out of the wood while cooking."

INGREDIENTS

1 (10 pound) whole turkey, neck and giblets removed

4 cloves garlic, crushed

2 tablespoons seasoned salt

1/2 cup butter

2 (12 fluid ounce) cans cola-flavored carbonated beverage

1 apple, quartered

1 onion, quartered

1 tablespoon garlic powder

1 tablespoon salt

1 tablespoon ground black pepper

DIRECTIONS

1. Preheat an outdoor smoker to 225 to 250°F (110 to 120°C).

2. Rinse turkey under cold water, and pat dry. Rub the crushed garlic over the outside of the bird, and sprinkle with seasoned salt. Place in a medium roasting pan. Fill turkey cavity with butter, cola, apple, onion, garlic powder, salt, and ground black pepper. Cover loosely with foil.

3. Smoke at 225 to 250°F (110 to 120°C) for 10 hours, or until internal temperature reaches 180°F (80°C) when measured in the thigh meat. Baste the bird every 1 to 2 hours with the juices from the bottom of the roasting pan.

Cranberry Stuffed Turkey Breasts

Submitted by: **Esther Nelson**

Makes: 10 servings

Preparation: 1 hour

Cooking: 1 hour 10 minutes

Ready In: 2 hours 25 minutes

"I made these once for a holiday dinner party, and they were such a hit that I started making them for Thanksgiving instead of a whole turkey."

INGREDIENTS

1 (12 ounce) package herb-seasoned bread stuffing mix

2 skinless boneless turkey breasts

1 cup chopped pecans

2 (8 ounce) packages dried, sweetened cranberries

2 tablespoons olive oil

6 curly leaf lettuce leaves

1/2 cup pecan halves

DIRECTIONS

1. Preheat the oven to 350°F (175°C). Prepare stuffing mix according to package directions. Set aside to cool.

2. With a sharp knife, butterfly breasts open to lay flat. Place each breast between two sheets of waxed paper, and flatten with a mallet. Spread the prepared stuffing to within ¼ inch of the edge of each breast. Sprinkle each one with chopped pecans and dried cranberries, reserving some of the cranberries for garnish. Roll up tightly in a jellyroll style, starting with the long end. Tuck in ends, and tie in sections with string, about 4 sections around the middle and one running the length of the roll to secure the ends.

3. Heat olive oil in a large cast iron skillet over medium-high heat. Carefully brown rolls on all sides.

4. Place skillet in oven, uncovered. Bake in a preheated 350°F (175°C) oven for 1 hour, or until the internal temperature is at 170°F (78°C) when taken with a meat thermometer. Do not let these get overly dry.

5. Allow rolls to set for 15 minutes before removing string, and slicing into ½ to ¾ inch circles. Leave one roll whole, and slice the other for presentation. Stuffing will be spiraled into meat. Present on your prettiest platter on a bed of curly lettuce, and garnish by sprinkling with the remaining ½ cup pecan halves and the reserved dried cranberries.

Prime Rib

Submitted by: **Dale**

Makes: 1 (10 pound) rib roast

Preparation: 10 minutes

Cooking: 2 hours 30 minutes

Ready In: 2 hours 40 minutes

"Prime rib roast the easy way. Tastes delicious!"

INGREDIENTS

1 (10 pound) prime rib roast

6 cloves garlic, sliced

salt and ground black pepper to taste

1/2 cup Dijon mustard

DIRECTIONS

1. Preheat the oven to 500°F (260°C).

2. Make slits all over the roast by pricking with a small knife. Insert slivers of sliced garlic. Season the roast with salt and pepper, then spread generously with mustard. Place on a rack in a roasting pan, and cover.

3. Roast for 60 minutes in the preheated oven. Turn off oven. Leave oven closed, and do not peek for 90 minutes. The internal temperature of the meat should be at least 140°F (60°C) for medium-rare, or 155°F (68°C) for medium.

Prime Rib Roast

Submitted by: **William Anatooskin**

Makes: 1 (8 pound) roast

Preparation: 15 minutes

Cooking: 2 hours

Ready In: 4 hours 15 minutes

"This very flavorful roast is appropriate for any special occasion. The marinade in this recipe tenderizes the roast and the leftovers make fantastic sandwiches."

INGREDIENTS

3 teaspoons grated fresh ginger root

1/3 cup orange marmalade

4 cloves garlic, minced

3 tablespoons soy sauce

2 tablespoons brown sugar

1/4 teaspoon hot pepper sauce

1 tablespoon mustard powder

1 cup beer

1 (8 pound) prime rib roast

1/4 cup olive oil

ground black pepper to taste

DIRECTIONS

1. Mix together the ginger, marmalade, garlic, soy sauce, brown sugar, hot sauce, and mustard. Stir in the beer. Prick holes all over the roast with a 2 pronged fork. Pour marinade over roast. Cover, and refrigerate for at least 2 hours, basting at least twice.

2. Preheat oven to 400°F (200°C).

3. Place roast on a rack in a roasting pan. Pour about 1 cup of marinade into the roasting pan, and discard remaining marinade. Pour olive oil over roast, and season with freshly ground black pepper. Insert a roasting thermometer into the middle of the roast, making sure that the thermometer does not touch any bone. Cover roasting pan with aluminum foil, and seal edges tightly around pan.

4. Cook roast for 1 hour in the preheated oven. After the first hour, remove the aluminum foil. Baste, reduce heat to 325°F (165°C), and continue roasting for 1 more hour. The thermometer reading should be at least 140°F (60°C) for medium-rare, and 170°F (76°C) for well done. Remove roasting pan from oven, place aluminum foil over roast, and let rest for about 30 minutes before slicing.

Sangria Ham

Submitted by: **Mary Glenn**

Makes: 1 (8 pound) ham

Preparation: 20 minutes

Cooking: 4 hours

Ready In: 4 hours 20 minutes

"This recipe requires four hours and twenty minutes, and results in the most delicious ham I have ever tasted. Burgundy wine may easily be substituted for the sangria and other fruit juices may be added to the blend but the acidity of the pineapple juice and the wine combination is hard to beat for tender moist ham."

INGREDIENTS

1 (8 pound) bone-in fresh ham with rind removed

1/4 cup whole cloves

1 pound brown sugar

1 cup unsweetened pineapple juice

2 cups sangria wine

DIRECTIONS

1. Preheat oven to 400°F (200°C).

2. Use a sharp knife to score the ham 1/4 inch deep in a diamond pattern. Place in a good sized roaster with the fat side up, and stud in a decorative manner with the whole cloves...be sure to use plenty. Pack the top of the ham with the whole pound of brown sugar to coat the surface as thickly as possible. Some may fall off into the pan, but that can not be helped. Leave it there to sweeten the basting juices needed in later steps.

3. Roast, uncovered, until the sugar begins to melt, about 20 minutes. During this time, mix together the pineapple juice and sangria. When the sugar has begun to melt, pour one cup of the wine mixture over the ham, and return the ham to the oven for 40 minutes. I often tent the ham with foil at some point, but my mother never did.

4. After one hour in the oven, baste the ham with a second cup of the wine mixture, stirring it into the pan drippings. Return the ham to the oven for 2 more hours, basting after the first hour with the remaining wine mixture.

5. Lower the oven temperature to 325°F (165°C), and baste the ham every 20 minutes with the pan drippings for the final hour of cooking. A meat thermometer should read 160°F (65°C) before serving.

Roast Pork

Submitted by: **Chris Lipo**

Makes: 1 (6 lb) pork loin roast

Preparation: 10 minutes

Cooking: 3 hours 30 minutes

Ready In: 15 hours 40 minutes

"This recipe takes some preparation, but is worth it. It has a slight Caribbean taste to it."

INGREDIENTS

¹/₂ cup fresh lime juice

³/₄ cup soy sauce

³/₄ cup white sugar

1 teaspoon grated fresh ginger

2 cloves garlic, minced

2 teaspoons salt

1 (6 pound) boneless pork loin roast

1 large onion, sliced into thin rings

2 bay leaves

DIRECTIONS

1. In a medium bowl, mix together the lime juice, soy sauce, sugar, ginger, garlic, and salt until the sugar dissolves.

2. Place the loin of pork in a roasting pan, and scatter the onion rings and bay leaves over it. Pour lime-ginger mixture over the meat, and cover with plastic wrap. Refrigerate for 12 hours or so, turning every once in a while.

3. Preheat the oven to 325°F (165°C).

4. Roast, uncovered, for about 3½ hours; baste frequently with pan juices. For a well done roast, cook until the internal temperature of the roast is 160°F (70°C).

Tangy Honey Glazed Ham

Submitted by: **Sue**

Makes: 1 (10 pound) ham

Preparation: 15 minutes

Cooking: 2 hours 45 minutes

Ready In: 3 hours

"I came up with the glaze for this ham using ingredients on hand and it's the best I've ever tasted. If you have any glaze left over, you can add it to the pan drippings with a little flour or cornstarch and make a nice sauce to accompany the meat. Use the bone and ham trimmings to make soup afterwards."

INGREDIENTS

1 (10 pound) fully-cooked, bone-in ham

1¹/4 cups packed dark brown sugar

¹/3 cup pineapple juice

¹/3 cup honey

¹/3 large orange, juiced and zested

2 tablespoons Dijon mustard

¹/4 teaspoon ground cloves

DIRECTIONS

1. Preheat oven to 325°F (165°C). Place ham in a roasting pan.

2. In a small saucepan, combine brown sugar, pineapple juice, honey, orange juice, orange zest, Dijon mustard, and ground cloves. Bring to a boil, reduce heat, and simmer for 5 to 10 minutes. Set aside.

3. Bake ham in preheated oven uncovered for 2 hours. Remove ham from oven, and brush with glaze. Bake for an additional 30 to 45 minutes, brushing ham with glaze every 10 minutes.

Roast Duck with Apple Dressing

Submitted by: **Debbie**

Makes: 4 servings

Preparation: 10 minutes

Cooking: 1 hour 20 minutes

Ready In: 1 hour 30 minutes

"When you're in the mood for something rich and flavorful, try this wild duck rubbed with light seasoning and stuffed with apples, celery and onion."

INGREDIENTS

1 (4 pound) whole duck

salt and pepper to taste

1 teaspoon poultry seasoning

1/2 tablespoon butter

3 tablespoons chopped onion

5 stalks celery, chopped

3 cups peeled, cored and chopped apple

3 cups cornbread crumbs

1 tablespoon olive oil

DIRECTIONS

1. Rinse duck and pat dry; rub with salt, pepper, and poultry seasoning.

2. Melt butter in a small skillet over medium heat. Saute onion and celery in butter until tender. In a medium bowl, combine with apple and cornbread crumbs. Mix together to make dressing (if necessary, add a little water to moisten).

3. Preheat oven to 350°F (175°C).

4. Fill the duck's cavity with dressing, and sew shut with kitchen twine. Rub outside of bird lightly with olive oil, and place in a shallow roasting pan or 9x13 inch baking dish.

5. Bake in preheated oven for 60 to 80 minutes, or until internal temperature reaches 180°F (80°C.)

Alaska Salmon Bake with Pecan Crunch Coating

Submitted by: **Chris Lipo**

Makes: 6 servings

Preparation: 20 minutes

Cooking: 10 minutes

Ready In: 30 minutes

"Baked salmon makes an excellent Christmas main course!"

INGREDIENTS

3 tablespoons Dijon mustard

3 tablespoons butter, melted

5 teaspoons honey

$1/2$ cup fresh bread crumbs

$1/2$ cup finely chopped pecans

3 teaspoons chopped fresh parsley

6 (4 ounce) fillets salmon

salt and pepper to taste

6 lemon wedges

DIRECTIONS

1. Preheat the oven to 400°F (200°C). In a small bowl, mix together the mustard, butter, and honey. In another bowl, mix together the bread crumbs, pecans, and parsley.

2. Season each salmon fillet with salt and pepper. Place on a lightly greased baking sheet. Brush with mustard-honey mixture. Cover the top of each fillet with bread crumb mixture.

3. Bake for 10 minutes per inch of thickness, measured at thickest part, or until salmon just flakes when tested with a fork. Serve garnished with lemon wedges.

Deep South Fried Chicken

Submitted by: **Marilyn**

Makes: 8 servings

Preparation: 10 minutes

Cooking: 35 minutes

Ready In: 45 minutes

"This was my grandmother's and mother's recipe. It is 125 plus years old. If you are going to fry anything, let it be a frying size chicken. Cut your calories some other way! Start a new tradition, as I have, of fried chicken on Christmas Day!"

INGREDIENTS

1 cup shortening

2 cups all-purpose flour

1 teaspoon salt

1 teaspoon ground black pepper

1 (2 to 3 pound) whole chicken, cut into pieces

DIRECTIONS

1. Heat the shortening in a large, cast iron skillet over medium-high heat.

2. In a brown paper lunch bag, combine the flour, salt, and pepper. Shake two chicken pieces in the bag to coat, and place them in the skillet. Repeat until all of the chicken is coated and in the skillet.

3. Fry the chicken over medium-high heat until all of the pieces have been browned on both sides. Turn the heat to medium-low, cover, and cook for 25 minutes. Remove the lid, and increase heat to medium-high. Continue frying until chicken pieces are a deep golden brown, and the juices run clear.

Christmas Eve Beef Stew

Submitted by: **Maridele Neikirk**

Makes: 8 servings

Preparation: 10 minutes

Cooking: 6 hours

Ready In: 6 hours 10 minutes

"This is a family tradition for Christmas Eve! Serve with a green salad and a loaf of warm bread. It can also be made in a slow cooker."

INGREDIENTS

2^1/$_2$ pounds beef stew meat, diced into 1 inch pieces

1 (28 ounce) can stewed tomatoes, with juice

1 cup chopped celery

4 carrots, sliced

3 potatoes, cubed

3 onions, chopped

3^1/$_2$ tablespoons tapioca

2 cubes beef bouillon

^{1}/$_8$ teaspoon dried thyme

^{1}/$_8$ teaspoon dried rosemary

^{1}/$_8$ teaspoon dried marjoram

^{1}/$_4$ cup red wine

2 cups water

1 (10 ounce) package frozen green peas, thawed

DIRECTIONS

1. Preheat the oven to 250°F (120°C).

2. Place beef, tomatoes, celery, carrots, potatoes, onions, and tapioca into a Dutch oven. Season with beef bouillon, thyme, rosemary, and marjoram, and stir in red wine and water.

3. Bake in the Dutch oven at 250°F (120°C) for 5 to 6 hours. Add peas during last half hour of cooking.

stuffings and breads

From the elaborate fruit-and-nut cornbread dressings to the classic sage and celery variety, no Thanksgiving or Christmas table is complete without a dish piled high with your favorite stuffing. Steaming, hot rolls will also be a welcome visitor. Nothing says, *I love you* like fresh baked goods coming out of the oven on a chilly winter's day.

Cranberry, Sausage and Apple Stuffing

Submitted by: **Ibby**

Makes: 12 servings

Preparation: 35 minutes

Cooking: 1 hour

Ready In: 1 hour 35 minutes

"A mellow stuffing that pairs up perfectly with the Roast Turkey with Maple Herb Butter and Gravy. If leeks are not available, substitute 4 cups chopped onions."

INGREDIENTS

12 cups white bread cubes

1 pound sweet Italian sausage, casings removed

1/4 cup butter

6 cups coarsely chopped leeks

2 tart green apples - peeled, cored and chopped

2 cups chopped celery

4 teaspoons poultry seasoning

2 teaspoons dried rosemary, chopped

1 cup dried cranberries

1 1/3 cups chicken broth

salt and pepper to taste

DIRECTIONS

1. Preheat oven to 350°F (175°C). Spread bread cubes in a single layer over two baking sheets. Bake until slightly dry, about 15 minutes.

2. In a large skillet over medium heat, cook sausage, crumbling coarsely, for about 10 minutes or until evenly brown. Drain off grease, and transfer sausage to a large bowl.

3. Melt butter in the skillet; add leeks, apples, celery, and poultry seasoning. Cook, stirring frequently, for about 10 minutes. Stir in the rosemary and dried cranberries.

4. Mix leek mixture and bread cubes with sausage in bowl. Spoon stuffing into turkey, packing loosely.

5. Bake remaining stuffing in a buttered baking dish, covered, at 350°F (175°C) for about 45 minutes. Uncover, and bake another 15 minutes to brown top.

Wild Mushroom Stuffing

Submitted by: **Christine**

Makes: 16 servings

Preparation: 1 hour

Cooking: 1 hour 50 minutes

Ready In: 2 hours 50 minutes

"The stuffing of the Pacific Northwest! You can fill your turkey with this stuffing, or bake it separately."

INGREDIENTS

2 cups hot water

1 ounce dried porcini mushrooms

1³/₄ pounds egg bread - crust trimmed, and cut into ³/₄ inch cubes

1 cup chopped hazelnuts

6 tablespoons unsalted butter

3 leeks, coarsely chopped

1 cup chopped shallots

1¹/₄ pounds crimini mushrooms, sliced

¹/₂ pound shiitake mushrooms, sliced

2 cups chopped celery

1 cup chopped fresh parsley

3 tablespoons chopped fresh thyme

2 tablespoons chopped fresh sage

salt and pepper to taste

2 eggs, lightly beaten

³/₄ cup chicken broth

DIRECTIONS

1. Soak porcini mushrooms in 2 cups hot water until the mushrooms are soft, about 30 minutes. Reserve soaking liquid, and chop mushrooms coarsely.

2. Preheat oven to 325°F (165°C). Arrange bread cubes on baking sheets in a single layer. Bake until beginning to brown, about 15 minutes. Spread hazelnuts in a single layer on a baking sheet. Toast for 8 to 10 minutes, or until lightly browned.

3. Melt butter in a Dutch oven over medium heat. Cook leeks, shallots, and crimini and shiitake mushrooms in the butter until tender, about 15 minutes. Mix in celery and porcini mushrooms, and cook for 5 minutes. Transfer to a large bowl, and mix with toasted bread cubes and nuts. Season with parsley, thyme, sage, salt, and pepper. Stir in beaten eggs. Combine broth and ¾ cup reserved porcini soaking liquid; add just enough broth mixture to the stuffing to moisten.

4. Transfer stuffing to a buttered 10x15 inch baking dish. Cover with buttered foil, and bake in preheated oven until heated through, about 1 hour. Uncover, and bake until top is crisp, about 15 minutes.

Awesome Sausage, Apple and Cranberry Stuffing

Submitted by: **Stacy M. Polcyn**

Makes: 10 servings

Preparation: 15 minutes

Cooking: 25 minutes

Ready In: 1 hour 40 minutes

"This Thanksgiving stuffing is fantastic! It is very flavorful and fresh-tasting. This recipe will stuff a 10-pound turkey (which serves six) plus extra. I replaced the usual pork sausage with much healthier turkey sausage. Other dried fruits may also be used in place of cranberries."

INGREDIENTS

1¹/2 cups cubed whole wheat bread

3³/4 cups cubed white bread

1 pound ground turkey sausage

1 cup chopped onion

³/4 cup chopped celery

2¹/2 teaspoons dried sage

1¹/2 teaspoons dried rosemary

¹/2 teaspoon dried thyme

1 Golden Delicious apple, cored and chopped

³/4 cup dried cranberries

¹/3 cup minced fresh parsley

1 cooked turkey liver, finely chopped

³/4 cup turkey stock

4 tablespoons unsalted butter, melted

DIRECTIONS

1. Preheat oven to 350 degree°F (175 degree°C). Spread the white and whole wheat bread cubes in a single layer on a large baking sheet. Bake for 5 to 7 minutes in the preheated oven, or until evenly toasted. Transfer toasted bread cubes to a large bowl.

2. In a large skillet, cook the sausage and onions over medium heat, stirring and breaking up the lumps until evenly browned. Add the celery, sage, rosemary, and thyme; cook, stirring, for 2 minutes to blend flavors.

3. Pour sausage mixture over bread in bowl. Mix in chopped apples, dried cranberries, parsley, and liver. Drizzle with turkey stock and melted butter, and mix lightly. Spoon into turkey to loosely fill.

Bread and Celery Stuffing

Submitted by: **Carlota Chmielewski**

Makes: 10 servings

Preparation: 20 minutes

Cooking: 40 minutes

Ready In: 2 hours

"An easy stuffing recipe for a 10 to 12 pound turkey."

INGREDIENTS

1 (1 pound) loaf sliced white bread

3/4 cup butter or margarine

1 onion, chopped

4 stalks celery, chopped

2 teaspoons poultry seasoning

salt and pepper to taste

1 cup chicken broth

DIRECTIONS

1. Let bread slices air dry for 1 to 2 hours, then cut into cubes.

2. In a Dutch oven, melt butter or margarine over medium heat. Cook onion and celery until soft. Season with poultry seasoning, salt, and pepper. Stir in bread cubes until evenly coated. Moisten with chicken broth; mix well.

3. Chill, and use as a stuffing for turkey, or bake in a buttered casserole dish at 350°F (175°C) for 30 to 40 minutes.

Grandma Ruth's Stuffing

Submitted by: **Ilene F.**

Makes: 16 servings

Preparation: 30 minutes

Ready In: 30 minutes

"This is a very basic and simple stuffing recipe that my Grandma Ruth was famous for. You can easily replace the eggs with an egg substitute with no notice-able taste difference. My family does not, but you can easily add cooked bulk sausage to this stuffing. For a moist stuffing made outside of the bird, add addi-tional chicken stock and cover with foil while baking. Remove foil for the last 20 minutes to crisp up the top."

INGREDIENTS

2 tablespoons olive oil

1 pound sliced fresh mushrooms

3 stalks celery, diced

2 onions, chopped

1 (20 ounce) loaf French or Italian bread, cut into 1 inch cubes

1 (16 ounce) package herb-seasoned stuffing mix

4 eggs, beaten

2 (14 ounce) cans chicken broth

2 teaspoons rubbed sage

2 teaspoons dried thyme

2 tablespoons garlic powder

salt and pepper to taste

DIRECTIONS

1. Heat oil in a large skillet over medium heat. Saute the mushrooms, celery, and onions until softened.

2. Dampen the fresh bread cubes (not the stuffing mix,) then squeeze out any excess water.

3. In a large bowl, combine the mushroom mixture, bread cubes, stuffing mix, eggs, and 1 can chicken broth. Season with sage, thyme, garlic powder, salt, and pepper, and mix well. The stuffing should have a rather paste-like consistency. Mix in additional chicken broth as necessary.

4. Loosely pack stuffing inside turkey cavity before roasting.

Slow Cooker Stuffing

Submitted by: **Gayle Wagner**

Makes: 8 servings

Preparation: 30 minutes

Cooking: 4 hours

Ready In: 4 hours 30 minutes

"This is an easy way to make 'extra' stuffing for a large crowd, saving stove space because it cooks in a slow cooker. Very tasty and moist!"

INGREDIENTS

1 cup butter or margarine

2 cups chopped onion

2 cups chopped celery

1/4 cup chopped fresh parsley

12 ounces sliced mushrooms

12 cups dry bread cubes

1 1/2 teaspoons dried sage

1 teaspoon dried thyme

1/2 teaspoon dried marjoram

1 teaspoon poultry seasoning

1 1/2 teaspoons salt

1/2 teaspoon ground black pepper

2 eggs, beaten

4 1/2 cups chicken broth, or as needed

DIRECTIONS

1. Melt butter in a skillet over medium heat. Saute onion, celery, mushrooms, and parsley until onions are soft. Place in a large bowl, and mix with bread cubes. Season with sage, thyme, marjoram, poultry seasoning, salt, and pepper. Toss until evenly coated. Add beaten eggs, and mix together. Pour in enough broth to moisten (3 to 4½ cups, depending on how dry your bread cubes are.)

2. Spoon stuffing into slow cooker, and cover. Set to High for 45 minutes.

3. Reduce to Low, and cook for 4 to 8 hours.

Apple Pecan Cornbread Dressing

Submitted by: **Walsie**

Makes: 10 cups

Preparation: 15 minutes

Cooking: 40 minutes

Ready In: 55 minutes

"Savory, yet sweet, this cornbread dressing will satisfy anyone's appetite. 2 teaspoons dried parsley flakes can be substituted for fresh parsley."

INGREDIENTS

1 (9x9 inch) pan cornbread, cooled and crumbled

1 (8 ounce) package herb-seasoned dry bread stuffing mix

2 tablespoons chopped fresh parsley

1/2 teaspoon ground ginger

1/2 teaspoon salt

3/4 cup butter

1 cup chopped celery

1 cup chopped onion

2 cups chopped apples

1/2 cup chopped pecans

2 cups apple juice

3 eggs, beaten

DIRECTIONS

1. Preheat oven to 350°F (175°C). Butter a 3 quart casserole dish.

2. Melt the butter in a heavy saucepan, and saute the celery and onion for 8 to 10 minutes, or until tender.

3. In a large bowl, combine the cornbread, stuffing mix, parsley, ginger, and salt. Mix in the celery and onion mixture, chopped apple, chopped pecans, apple juice, and beaten eggs. Spoon dressing into prepared casserole dish.

4. Bake for 30 to 35 minutes in the preheated oven, or until heated through, and lightly browned on top.

Holiday Dressing

Submitted by: **Louise Day**

Makes: 16 servings

Preparation: 20 minutes

Cooking: 2 hours

Ready In: 2 hours 45 minutes

"This recipe was given to me by my friend Gloria 15 years ago. I have used it ever since then. No other dressing will serve the purpose, according to my adult son."

INGREDIENTS

1 (7.5 ounce) package dry cornbread mix

1 cup butter

2 onions, chopped

1 green bell pepper, chopped

6 stalks celery, chopped

1 pound pork sausage

16 slices white bread

2 teaspoons dried sage

1 teaspoon dried thyme

1 teaspoon poultry seasoning

1 teaspoon salt

$1/2$ teaspoon ground black pepper

$1/2$ cup chopped fresh parsley

2 eggs

4 cups chicken stock

DIRECTIONS

1. Prepare corn bread as directed on package. Cool, and crumble.

2. Melt butter in a large skillet over medium heat. Cook onions, bell pepper, and celery in butter until tender, but not brown. In another pan, cook sausage over medium-high heat until evenly browned.

3. Place corn bread and bread slices in a food processor. Pulse until they turn into a crumbly mixture. Transfer mixture to a large bowl. Season with sage, thyme, poultry seasoning, salt, and pepper. Mix in chopped parsley, cooked vegetables, and sausage with drippings. Stir in eggs and chicken stock. This mixture should be a bit mushy. Transfer to a greased 9x13 inch pan.

4. Bake at 325°F (165°C) for 1 hour.

Ibby's Pumpkin Mushroom Stuffing

Submitted by: Ibby

Makes: 8 servings

Preparation: 1 hour 30 minutes

Cooking: 1 hour

Ready In: 2 hours 30 minutes

"A dark and wild tasting stuffing that is sure to disappear quickly!"

INGREDIENTS

6 cups cubed pumpkin bread

1 cup chopped celery

1 cup butter or margarine

2 cups chopped red onion

2 cups sliced crimini mushrooms

2 tablespoons chopped fresh rosemary

2 tablespoons chopped fresh tarragon

2 tablespoons chopped fresh chives

2 tablespoons chopped fresh parsley

1 1/2 teaspoons salt

1 teaspoon ground black pepper

6 tablespoons chicken broth

DIRECTIONS

1. Spread bread cubes on a baking sheet, and let dry overnight. Alternatively, heat in a 250°F (120°C) oven until dry, about 1 hour.

2. Preheat oven to 375°F (190°C). Butter a 2 quart baking dish.

3. Melt butter in a large skillet over medium heat. Saute celery and onions for about 10 minutes. Add mushrooms, and continue cooking for about 8 minutes, or until tender. Season with rosemary, tarragon, chives, parsley, salt, and pepper. Fold in bread cubes, and add enough broth to moisten. Transfer to prepared dish, and cover with foil.

4. Bake in preheated oven for 40 minutes. Remove cover, and bake for 10 minutes, or until top is crisp.

Fresh Herb Dinner Rolls

Submitted by: **Stephano**

Makes: 2 dozen

Preparation: 30 minutes

Cooking: 30 minutes

Ready In: 2 hours

"Soft and tender dinner rolls with the wonderful smell of fresh herbs."

INGREDIENTS

1 (.25 ounce) package active dry yeast

1 tablespoon white sugar

1 cup warm water (110 degrees F/45 degrees C)

1 cup milk, room temperature

2 eggs

2 teaspoons salt

2 tablespoons butter, softened

1/4 cup chopped fresh parsley

1/4 cup chopped fresh chives

6 cups bread flour

1 egg white

2 tablespoons water

DIRECTIONS

1. In a small mixing bowl, dissolve yeast and sugar in 1 cup warm water. Let stand until creamy; about 10 minutes.

2. In a large bowl, stir together the yeast mixture with milk, eggs, salt, butter, parsley, chives, and 4 cups flour. Add the remaining flour, ½ cup at a time, until dough has pulled together. Turn dough out onto a lightly floured surface, and knead until smooth and elastic, about 8 minutes. Lightly oil a large bowl, place the dough in the bowl, and turn to coat with oil. Cover with a damp cloth and put in a warm place to rise until doubled in volume, about 1 hour.

3. Grease two 9x13 inch baking pans. Deflate the dough, and turn it out onto a lightly floured surface. Divide the dough into 24 pieces. Shape each piece into a round ball, and place into the prepared pans. Cover the rolls with a warm, damp cloth, and let rise until doubled in volume, about 40 minutes.

4. Preheat oven to 350°F (175°C). In a small bowl, lightly beat the egg white with 2 tablespoons of water; brush egg wash over tops of rolls.

5. Bake in preheated oven for about 30 minutes, or until golden brown.

Colleen's Potato Crescent Rolls

Submitted by: **Colleen Wollenberg**

Makes: 32 rolls

Preparation: 30 minutes

Cooking: 30 minutes

Ready In: 9 hours 40 minutes

"Between family, friends and co-workers, I get requests for these rolls about every weekend. They have a terrific flavor! Mix garlic or cinnamon into the butter topping for more variety."

INGREDIENTS

2 potatoes, peeled and cut into 1 inch cubes

1 (.25 ounce) package active dry yeast

1 1/2 cups warm water (110 degrees F/45 degrees C)

2/3 cup white sugar

2/3 cup shortening

2 eggs

1 1/2 teaspoons salt

6 1/2 cups all-purpose flour

1/4 cup butter, melted

DIRECTIONS

1. Place potatoes in a saucepan, and cover with water. Bring to a boil, and cook until tender, about 15 minutes. Drain, cool, and mash.

2. In a large bowl, dissolve yeast in warm water. Let stand until creamy, about 10 minutes.

3. When yeast is ready, mix in 1 cup mashed potatoes, sugar, shortening, eggs, salt, and 3 cups flour. Stir in the remaining flour, 1/2 cup at a time, until dough has become stiff but still pliable. Turn dough out onto a lightly floured surface, and knead until smooth and elastic, about 8 minutes. Lightly oil a large bowl, place the dough in the bowl, and turn to coat with oil. Cover with plastic wrap, and refrigerate for at least 8 hours, and up to 5 days.

4. Deflate the dough, and turn it out onto a lightly floured surface. Divide the dough into two equal pieces, and form into rounds. Roll out each round to a 12 inch circle. Brush generously with melted butter, and cut each circle into 16 wedges. Roll wedges up tightly, starting with the large end. Place on lightly greased baking sheets with the points underneath, and the ends bent to form a crescent shape. Cover, and let rise for 1 hour. Meanwhile, preheat oven to 400°F (200°C).

5. Bake in preheated oven for 15 to 20 minutes, or until golden brown.

French Bread Rolls to Die For

Submitted by: **Jo Catlin**

Makes: 16 rolls

Preparation: 20 minutes

Cooking: 20 minutes

Ready In: 2 hours 20 minutes

"Easy to make French bread rolls. Dough can be made in mixer, bread maker, or by hand. Loaves or rolls can be brushed before baking with a glaze of 1 beaten egg white mixed with 1 tablespoon water if desired."

INGREDIENTS

1¹/₂ cups warm water (110 degrees F/45 degrees C)

1 tablespoon active dry yeast

2 tablespoons white sugar

2 tablespoons vegetable oil

1 teaspoon salt

4 cups bread flour

DIRECTIONS

1. In a large bowl, stir together warm water, yeast, and sugar. Let stand until creamy, about 10 minutes.

2. To the yeast mixture, add the oil, salt, and 2 cups flour. Stir in the remaining flour, ½ cup at a time, until the dough has pulled away from the sides of the bowl. Turn out onto a lightly floured surface, and knead until smooth and elastic, about 8 minutes. Lightly oil a large bowl, place the dough in the bowl, and turn to coat. Cover with a damp cloth, and let rise in a warm place until doubled in volume, about 1 hour.

3. Deflate the dough, and turn it out onto a lightly floured surface. Divide the dough into 16 equal pieces, and form into round balls. Place on lightly greased baking sheets at least 2 inches apart. Cover the rolls with a damp cloth, and let rise until doubled in volume, about 40 minutes. Meanwhile, preheat oven to 400°F (200°C).

4. Bake for 18 to 20 minutes in the preheated oven, or until golden brown.

Light Wheat Rolls

Submitted by: **Susan Harshbarger**

Makes: 2 dozen

Preparation: 30 minutes

Cooking: 15 minutes

Ready In: 3 hours 5 minutes

"This is a yummy recipe for a light wheat roll that I keep in my special book of most liked recipes. They are not complicated at all to make, just a lot of rising time."

INGREDIENTS

2 (.25 ounce) packages active dry yeast

1³/₄ cups warm water (110 degrees F/45 degrees C)

¹/₂ cup white sugar

1 teaspoon salt

¹/₄ cup butter, melted and cooled

1 egg, beaten

2¹/₄ cups whole wheat flour

2¹/₂ cups all-purpose flour

¹/₄ cup butter, melted

DIRECTIONS

1. In a large bowl, dissolve yeast in warm water. Let stand until creamy, about 10 minutes.

2. Mix sugar, salt, ¼ cup melted butter, egg, and whole wheat flour into yeast mixture. Stir in all-purpose flour, ½ cup at a time, until dough pulls away from the sides of the bowl. Turn dough out onto a well floured surface, and knead until smooth and elastic, about 8 minutes. Lightly oil a large bowl, place dough in bowl, and turn to coat. Cover with a damp cloth, and let rise in a warm place until doubled in volume, about 1 hour.

3. Punch down dough, cover, and let rise in warm place until doubled again, about 30 minutes.

4. Grease 2 dozen muffin cups. Punch down dough, and divide into two equal portions. Roll each into a 6x14 inch rectangle, and cut rectangle into twelve 7x1 inch strips. Roll strips up into spirals, and place into muffin cups. Brush tops with melted butter. Let rise uncovered in a warm place 40 minutes, or until doubled in bulk.

5. Preheat oven to 400°F (200°C). Bake for 12 to 15 minutes, or until golden brown. Remove from oven, and brush again with melted butter.

Bread Machine Rolls

Submitted by: **Kay**

Makes: 1 dozen rolls

Preparation: 1 hour 20 minutes

Cooking: 15 minutes

Ready In: 1 hour 35 minutes

"These are the BEST dinner rolls I've ever made. They also make great buns for sandwiches. For a festive presentation, sprinkle with poppy or sesame seeds before baking."

INGREDIENTS

3 cups bread flour

3 tablespoons white sugar

1 teaspoon salt

¼ cup dry milk powder

1 cup warm water (110 degrees F/45 degrees C)

2 tablespoons butter, softened

1 (.25 ounce) package active dry yeast

1 egg white

2 tablespoons water

DIRECTIONS

1. Place the bread flour, sugar, salt, milk powder, water, butter, and yeast in the pan of the bread machine in the order recommended by the manufacturer. Set on Dough cycle; press Start.

2. Remove risen dough from the machine, deflate, and turn out onto a lightly floured surface. Divide the dough into twelve equal pieces, and form into rounds. Place the rounds on lightly greased baking sheets. Cover the rolls with a damp cloth, and let rise until doubled in volume, about 40 minutes. Meanwhile, preheat oven to 350°F (175°C).

3. In a small bowl, mix together the egg white and 2 tablespoons water; brush lightly onto the rolls. Bake in the preheated oven for 15 minutes, or until the rolls are golden brown.

Butterhorn Rolls

Submitted by: **Ricki Heronemus**

Makes: 32 rolls

Preparation: 20 minutes

Cooking: 10 minutes

Ready In: 12 hours 30 minutes

"Cool rise rolls, let rise overnight, no kneading needed."

INGREDIENTS

1 cup shortening

1 cup milk

1¹/₂ teaspoons active dry yeast

1 teaspoon white sugar

¹/₂ cup warm water (110 degrees F/45 degrees C)

2 eggs

¹/₂ cup white sugar

2 teaspoons salt

4¹/₂ cups all-purpose flour

1 teaspoon baking powder

¹/₂ cup butter, softened

DIRECTIONS

1. In a small saucepan, combine shortening and milk. Heat until shortening is melted; set aside to cool. Dissolve the yeast and 1 teaspoon sugar in the warm water. In a large bowl, beat the eggs, ½ cup sugar, and salt together. Add the milk mixture and yeast mixture to the egg mixture, stirring to blend. Sift in the flour and baking powder, and mix well. Cover, and refrigerate overnight.

2. Divide dough into fourths, and on a floured surface, roll out into ½ inch thick circles. Spread surface with the soft butter. Cut each circle like a pie into 8 triangles, and roll up from larger to small end. Place rolls point side down on a baking sheet, and allow to rise until doubled, 3 to 4 hours. Preheat oven to 400°F (200°C.)

3. Bake rolls for 8 to 10 minutes in the preheated oven, or until golden brown.

Butter Crescents

Submitted by: **Rita Fay**

Makes: 1 dozen rolls

Preparation: 30 minutes

Cooking: 15 minutes

Ready In: 2 hours 15 minutes

"Melt in your mouth crescent rolls! This recipe takes a little time but is well worth the wait."

INGREDIENTS

$^1/_2$ cup milk

$^1/_2$ cup butter, softened

$^1/_3$ cup white sugar

$^1/_2$ teaspoon salt

1 (.25 ounce) package active dry yeast

$^1/_2$ cup warm water (110 degrees F/45 degrees C)

1 egg

3$^1/_2$ cups all-purpose flour

1 egg, beaten

DIRECTIONS

1. Warm the milk in a small saucepan until bubbles form at the edges; remove from heat. Mix in the butter, sugar, and salt. Let cool until lukewarm. In a small bowl, dissolve yeast in warm water. Let stand until creamy, about 10 minutes.

2. In a large bowl, combine milk and yeast mixtures. Stir in 1 egg. Beat in flour 1 cup at a time until dough pulls together. Turn out onto a lightly floured surface, and knead until smooth and elastic, about 8 minutes. Lightly oil a large bowl, place the dough in the bowl, and turn to coat. Cover with a damp cloth, and let rise in a warm place until doubled in volume, about 1 hour.

3. Deflate the dough, and turn it out onto a lightly floured surface. Divide the dough into two equal pieces, and form into rounds. Cover, and let rest 10 minutes.

4. Using a floured rolling pin, roll each dough half into a 12 inch circle. Cut each circle into 6 wedges. Roll each wedge up towards the point. Bend ends inward to form crescents, and place point side down on lightly greased baking sheets. Cover, and let rise until doubled, about 30 minutes. Meanwhile, preheat oven to 400°F (200°C).

5. Brush rolls with beaten egg, and bake for 12 to 15 minutes in the preheated oven, or until golden brown.

Angel Biscuits II

Submitted by: **Karin Christian**

Makes: 2 dozen biscuits

Preparation: 35 minutes

Cooking: 10 minutes

Ready In: 1 hour 45 minutes

"These are a delicious cross between a roll and a biscuit. You roll them out like a biscuit, and they rise like a roll."

INGREDIENTS

1 (.25 ounce) package active dry yeast

1/4 cup warm water (110 degrees F/45 degrees C)

2 cups buttermilk

5 cups all-purpose flour

1 tablespoon baking powder

1 teaspoon baking soda

2 teaspoons salt

3 tablespoons white sugar

3/4 cup shortening

DIRECTIONS

1. In a small bowl, dissolve yeast in warm water. Let stand until creamy, about 5 minutes. Add buttermilk to yeast mixture, and set aside.

2. In a large bowl, combine flour, sugar, baking powder, baking soda, and salt. Cut in shortening with a pastry blender until mixture resembles coarse meal. Stir in yeast mixture until dry ingredients are moistened. Turn dough out onto a floured surface, and knead 4 or 5 times.

3. On a lightly floured surface, roll dough to ½ inch thickness. Cut out biscuits with a 2 ½ inch round cutter. Place on lightly greased baking sheets, barely touching each other. Cover, and let rise in a warm place free from drafts for 1 hour, or until almost doubled in size. Preheat oven to 425°F (220°C).

4. Bake in preheated oven for 10 to 12 minutes, or until browned.

Mayonnaise Biscuits

Submitted by: **Georgie Brent**

Makes: 1 dozen biscuits

Preparation: 10 minutes

Cooking: 12 minutes

Ready In: 22 minutes

"This is a simple but tasty biscuit recipe. You don't taste the mayo, but it gives the biscuits a light and fluffy texture. For rolled and cut biscuits, use just enough milk to hold it together."

INGREDIENTS

2 cups self-rising flour

1 cup milk

6 tablespoons mayonnaise

DIRECTIONS

1. Preheat oven to 400°F (200°C).

2. In a large bowl, stir together flour, milk, and mayonnaise until just blended. Drop by spoonfuls onto lightly greased baking sheets.

3. Bake for 12 minutes in the preheated oven, or until golden brown.

Cheddar Biscuits

Submitted by: **Chaney**

Makes: 8 biscuits

Preparation: 15 minutes

Cooking: 20 minutes

Ready In: 35 minutes

"This is a very tasty, easy bread to make. It goes great with things like spaghetti and lasagna."

INGREDIENTS

2 cups biscuit baking mix

1 cup shredded Cheddar cheese

2/3 cup milk

1/2 teaspoon garlic powder

2 tablespoons margarine, melted

2 teaspoons dried parsley

1 teaspoon garlic salt

DIRECTIONS

1. Preheat oven to 400°F (205°C). Grease a cookie sheet, or line with parchment paper.

2. In a large bowl, combine baking mix, Cheddar cheese, and garlic powder. Stir in milk. Drop batter by heaping tablespoonfuls onto prepared cookie sheet.

3. Bake in preheated oven for 10 minutes. Brush biscuits with melted margarine, and sprinkle with parsley and garlic salt. Bake for 5 more minutes, or until lightly browned on the bottom.

Corn Fritters

Submitted by: **Joan Zaffary**

Makes: 1 dozen fritters

Preparation: 10 minutes

Cooking: 20 minutes

Ready In: 30 minutes

"Nothing warms up a cool night like a plateful of old-time corn fritters! Dig in, these are delicious!"

INGREDIENTS

3 cups oil for frying

1 cup sifted all-purpose flour

1 teaspoon baking powder

1/2 teaspoon salt

1/4 teaspoon white sugar

1 egg, lightly beaten

1/2 cup milk

1 tablespoon shortening, melted

1 (12 ounce) can whole kernel corn, drained

DIRECTIONS

1. Heat oil in a heavy pot or deep fryer to 365°F (185°C).

2. In a medium bowl, combine flour, baking powder, salt and sugar. Beat together egg, milk, and melted shortening; stir into flour mixture. Mix in the corn kernels.

3. Drop fritter batter by spoonfuls into the hot oil, and fry until golden. Drain on paper towels.

side dishes

Every family has a specialty when it comes to holiday side dishes. From mashed potatoes to vegetable casseroles, each has a place of honor at the feast. Celebrate Thanksgiving with squash, yams, and mashed potatoes. Add color to the table with green beans, carrots, or a cheesy-broccoli casserole. These recipes will punctuate the event with their outstanding flavor and classic style.

Roasted Garlic Mashed Potatoes

Submitted by: **Barrett**

Makes: 8 servings

Preparation: 15 minutes

Cooking: 1 hour

Ready In: 1 hour 15 minutes

"It is the sweetness of the roasted garlic that makes these mashed potatoes so delicious."

INGREDIENTS

6 cloves garlic, peeled

¹⁄₄ cup olive oil

7 baking potatoes, peeled and cubed

¹⁄₂ cup milk

¹⁄₄ cup grated Parmesan cheese

2 tablespoons butter

¹⁄₂ teaspoon salt

¹⁄₄ teaspoon ground black pepper

DIRECTIONS

1. Preheat oven to 350°F (175°C).

2. Place garlic cloves in a small baking dish. Drizzle with olive oil, cover, and bake 45 minutes, or until golden brown.

3. Bring a large pot of lightly salted water to boil. Add potatoes, and cook until tender but firm. Drain, and transfer to a large mixing bowl.

4. Place roasted garlic, milk, Parmesan cheese, and butter into the bowl with the potatoes. Season with salt and pepper. Beat to desired consistency with an electric mixer.

Make-Ahead Mashed Potatoes

Submitted by: **Carol Evans**

Makes: 12 servings

Preparation: 15 minutes

Cooking: 1 hour 5 minutes

Ready In: 1 hour 20 minutes

"You can make these ahead several days and store in the fridge. If baking cold, let stand 30 minutes first."

INGREDIENTS

5 pounds Yukon Gold potatoes, cubed

2 (3 ounce) packages cream cheese

8 ounces sour cream

1/2 cup milk

2 teaspoons onion salt

ground black pepper to taste

DIRECTIONS

1. Preheat the oven to 325°F (165°C).

2. Place potatoes in a large pot of lightly salted water. Bring to a boil, and cook until tender, about 15 minutes. Drain, and mash.

3. In a large bowl, mix mashed potatoes, cream cheese, sour cream, milk, onion salt, and pepper. Transfer to a large casserole dish.

4. Cover, and bake for 50 minutes in the preheated oven.

Baked Mashed Potatoes

Submitted by: **Nancy F.**

Makes: 12 servings

Preparation: 20 minutes

Cooking: 1 hour 15 minutes

Ready In: 1 hour 35 minutes

"Mashed potatoes that are lighter and fluffier. Cream cheese gives them a richer flavor. Can be made ahead of time!"

INGREDIENTS

5 pounds Yukon Gold potatoes, peeled and cubed

1/2 cup butter

1/4 cup milk

1 (8 ounce) package cream cheese, softened

1 onion, grated

1 egg

salt and pepper to taste

DIRECTIONS

1. Preheat oven to 350°F (175°C).

2. Bring a large pot of lightly salted water to a boil. Add potatoes, and cook until tender but firm, about 15 minutes; drain.

3. In a large bowl, mash potatoes with the butter and milk. With a hand mixer, beat in cream cheese and onion. In a small bowl, beat the egg with a little bit of the mashed potatoes. Stir into potatoes, and season with salt and pepper. Transfer to a 2 quart casserole dish.

4. Bake 1 hour in the preheated oven, or until puffy and lightly browned.

Hashbrown Casserole

Submitted by: **Louise**

Makes: 10 servings

Preparation: 15 minutes

Cooking: 45 minutes

Ready In: 1 hour

"It is very easy to make, and everyone loves this casserole."

INGREDIENTS

2 (10.75 ounce) cans condensed cream of chicken soup

1¹/₂ cups sour cream

2 tablespoons butter, softened

2 tablespoons dried minced onion flakes

ground black pepper to taste

1 (2 pound) package frozen shredded hash brown potatoes, thawed

4 ounces extra sharp Cheddar cheese, shredded

¹/₂ cup crushed cornflakes cereal

DIRECTIONS

1. Preheat oven to 350°F (175°C). Lightly grease a 9x13 inch baking dish.

2. In a large bowl, mix together the soup, sour cream, butter, dried onion flakes, and pepper. Stir in the hash browns and ½ the cheese. Pour into the prepared baking dish, sprinkle with remaining cheese, and top with crushed cornflakes.

3. Bake 45 minutes in the preheated oven, or until cheese is melted and bubbly.

Cheesy Potatoes

Submitted by: **Holly Bobst**

Makes: 8 servings

Preparation: 15 minutes

Cooking: 1 hour 10 minutes

Ready In: 1 hour 25 minutes

"Another name for my scalloped potatoes, this cheesy dish is my husband's favorite!"

INGREDIENTS

8 medium baking potatoes, peeled and sliced

1 onion, chopped

1 (1 pound) loaf processed cheese food, sliced

1/2 cup butter, sliced

salt and pepper to taste

1 1/2 cups milk

DIRECTIONS

1. Preheat oven to 375°F (190°C).

2. Place ½ the potatoes in a medium baking dish. Layer with ½ of the onion, ½ of the processed cheese, and ½ of the butter. Season with salt and pepper. Repeat layers, reserving 5 or 6 slices of the processed cheese. Pour in milk to approximately 1 inch depth.

3. Bake 40 minutes in the preheated oven, stirring twice. Top with remaining cheese food, and continue baking 30 minutes, or until potatoes are tender.

Rosemary Mashed Potatoes and Yams

Submitted by: **Ibby**

Makes: 10 servings

Preparation: 20 minutes

Cooking: 1 hour 35 minutes

Ready In: 2 hours

"A twist on the traditional mashed potatoes."

INGREDIENTS

8 cloves garlic

3 tablespoons olive oil

1 1/2 pounds baking potatoes, peeled and cubed

1 1/2 pounds yams, peeled and cubed

1/2 cup milk

1/4 cup butter

1/2 teaspoon dried rosemary

1/2 cup grated Parmesan cheese

salt and pepper to taste

DIRECTIONS

1. Preheat oven to 350°F (175°C). Lightly grease an 8 inch square baking dish.

2. Place garlic in small ovenproof bowl, and drizzle with olive oil. Roast for 30 minutes, or until very soft. Cool and peel the garlic, and reserve the oil.

3. Boil potatoes and yams in a large pot of salted water until tender, about 20 minutes. Drain, reserving 1 cup liquid.

4. Place potatoes and yams in a large bowl with milk, butter, rosemary, garlic, and reserved olive oil. Mash to desired consistency, adding reserved cooking liquid as needed. Mix in 1/4 cup cheese. Season with salt and pepper to taste. Transfer to the prepared baking dish. Sprinkle with remaining cheese.

5. Bake until heated through and golden on top, about 45 minutes.

Southern Candied Sweet Potatoes

Submitted by: **Pam Reed**

Makes: 8 servings

Preparation: 15 minutes

Cooking: 1 hour 10 minutes

Ready In: 1 hour 25 minutes

"Traditional sweet potato recipe. It is usually served as a side dish."

INGREDIENTS

2 cups white sugar

1 teaspoon ground cinnamon

1 teaspoon ground nutmeg

1 pinch salt

$^1/_2$ cup butter

6 sweet potatoes, peeled and sliced

1 tablespoon vanilla extract

DIRECTIONS

1. In a small bowl, mix the sugar, cinnamon, nutmeg, and salt together.

2. Melt butter in a large skillet over medium heat; add sweet potatoes, and stir to coat. Sprinkle sugar mixture over the sweet potatoes, and stir. Cover skillet, and reduce heat to low. Cook, stirring occasionally, for 1 hour, or until the sauce is dark and the potatoes are candied. They should be tender, but a little hard around the edges.

3. Stir in vanilla, and serve.

Brandied Candied Sweet Potatoes

Submitted by: **Kathy Bennett**

Makes: 8 servings

Preparation: 15 minutes

Cooking: 30 minutes

Ready In: 45 minutes

"This has been a Thanksgiving favorite of ours for many years because it is different from the many mashed sweet potatoes recipes."

INGREDIENTS

2 pounds sweet potatoes, peeled and diced

1/2 cup butter

1/2 cup packed brown sugar

1/2 cup brandy

1/2 teaspoon salt

DIRECTIONS

1. Place sweet potatoes in a large saucepan with enough water to cover. Bring to a boil. Cook 15 minutes, or until tender but firm. Drain, and set aside.

2. In a large skillet over low heat, melt the butter. Stir in the brown sugar, brandy, and salt. Add the sweet potatoes, and stir to coat. Cook, stirring gently, until sweet potatoes are heated through and well glazed.

Baked Sweet Potatoes with Ginger and Honey

Makes: 12 servings

Preparation: 15 minutes

Cooking: 40 minutes

Ready In: 55 minutes

Submitted by: **Chris Lipo**

"Fresh ginger, cardamom, and sweet potatoes will fill your house with a fall fragrance as well as call your family to the table."

INGREDIENTS

3 pounds sweet potatoes, peeled and cubed

1/2 cup honey

3 tablespoons grated fresh ginger

2 tablespoons walnut oil

1 teaspoon ground cardamom

1/2 teaspoon ground black pepper

DIRECTIONS

1. Preheat oven to 400°F (200°C).

2. In a large bowl, toss together the sweet potatoes, honey, ginger, walnut oil, cardamom, and pepper. Transfer to a large cast iron frying pan.

3. Bake for 20 minutes in the preheated oven. Stir the potatoes to expose the pieces from the bottom of the pan. Bake for another 20 minutes, or until the sweet potatoes are tender and caramelized on the outside.

Gourmet Sweet Potato Classic

Submitted by: **Heather**

Makes: 8 servings

Preparation: 20 minutes

Cooking: 1 hour 5 minutes

Ready In: 1 hour 25 minutes

"Once you taste this, you won't ever go back to the marshmallow-topped variety! I have peeled and cooked in the microwave, and also boiled the sweet potatoes. They taste the same no matter how you cook them. So, use the technique that works best for you!"

INGREDIENTS

5 sweet potatoes

1/4 teaspoon salt

1/4 cup butter

2 eggs

1 teaspoon vanilla extract

1/2 teaspoon ground cinnamon

1/2 cup white sugar

2 tablespoons heavy cream

1/4 cup butter, softened

3 tablespoons all-purpose flour

3/4 cup packed light brown sugar

1/2 cup chopped pecans

DIRECTIONS

1. Preheat oven to 350°F (175°C). Lightly grease a 9x13 inch baking dish.

2. Bake sweet potatoes 35 minutes in the preheated oven, or until they begin to soften. Cool slightly, peel, and mash.

3. In a large bowl, mix the mashed sweet potatoes, salt, ¼ cup butter, eggs, vanilla extract, cinnamon, sugar, and heavy cream. Transfer to the prepared baking dish.

4. In a medium bowl, combine ¼ cup butter, flour, brown sugar, and chopped pecans. Mix with a pastry blender or your fingers to the consistency of course meal. Sprinkle over the sweet potato mixture.

5. Bake 30 minutes in the preheated oven, until topping is crisp and lightly browned.

Rum and Sweet Potato Casserole

Submitted by: **Casey Tudor**

Makes: 8 servings

Preparation: 20 minutes

Cooking: 45 minutes

Ready In: 1 hour 15 minutes

"This is a simple recipe for sweet potato casserole. But it is also the best I have tasted, enriched with eggs, milk, and rum, and topped with a crunchy pecan streusel. It is a standard at all holiday dinners in my family. The amount of rum can be varied according to taste (the casserole is also good without it)."

INGREDIENTS

3 cups mashed sweet potatoes

1 cup white sugar

2 eggs, beaten

1/2 cup milk

1 teaspoon vanilla extract

1/2 cup butter, melted

1/3 cup dark rum

1 cup brown sugar

1 cup chopped pecans

1/3 cup self-rising flour

1/3 cup butter, melted

DIRECTIONS

1. Preheat oven to 350°F (175°C). Grease a 9x13 inch baking dish.

2. In a large bowl, mix the sweet potatoes and sugar. Stir in the eggs. Mix in milk, vanilla extract, and 1/2 cup melted butter. Gradually stir in the rum until well blended. Transfer the mixture to the prepared baking dish.

3. In a medium bowl, mix the brown sugar, pecans, flour, and 1/3 cup melted butter. Sprinkle this mixture over the mashed sweet potato mixture.

4. Bake 30 minutes in the preheated oven. Allow to sit at least 10 minutes before serving.

Sweet Potato Casserole

Submitted by: **Nancy**

Makes: 8 servings

Preparation: 15 minutes

Cooking: 50 minutes

Ready In: 1 hour 5 minutes

"Sweet, rich, and crunchy. A lovely addition to your holiday feast."

INGREDIENTS

1 (40 ounce) can cut sweet potatoes, undrained

1 cup white sugar

2 eggs

1/3 cup butter

1/3 cup milk

1 teaspoon vanilla extract

1 cup packed brown sugar

1 cup chopped pecans

1/3 cup all-purpose flour

1/3 cup butter, melted

DIRECTIONS

1. Preheat oven to 350°F (175°C). Butter a 2 quart baking dish.

2. Place the sweet potatoes and their liquid in a medium saucepan, and bring to a boil. Cook 15 minutes, or until tender. Remove from heat, drain, and mash.

3. In a medium bowl, mix the mashed sweet potatoes, white sugar, eggs, 1/3 cup butter, milk, and vanilla extract. Spread evenly into the prepared baking dish.

4. In a separate bowl, mix the brown sugar, chopped pecans, flour, and 1/3 cup melted butter. Sprinkle over the sweet potato mixture.

5. Bake 35 minutes in the preheated oven, or until a knife inserted near the center comes out clean.

Sweet Potato Casserole II

Submitted by: **Stephanie Phillips**

Makes: 8 servings

Preparation: 15 minutes

Cooking: 45 minutes

Ready In: 1 hour

"Mmm! Sweet potatoes topped with creamy toasted marshmallows."

INGREDIENTS

5 sweet potatoes, sliced

1/4 cup reduced fat margarine

1/2 cup packed brown sugar

3 tablespoons orange juice

1 pinch ground cinnamon

1 (10.5 ounce) package miniature marshmallows

DIRECTIONS

1. Preheat oven to 350°F (175°C).

2. Place sweet potatoes in a large saucepan with enough water to cover. Bring to a boil, and cook until tender, about 15 minutes. Remove from heat, drain, and mash.

3. Place mashed sweet potatoes in large bowl, and use an electric mixer to blend with the margarine, brown sugar, orange juice, and cinnamon. Spread evenly into a 9x13 inch baking dish. Top with miniature marshmallows.

4. Bake for 25 to 30 minutes in the preheated oven, or until heated through, and marshmallows are puffed and golden brown.

Yam and Apple Casserole

Submitted by: **Lynn**

Makes: 8 servings

Preparation: 30 minutes

Cooking: 2 hours

Ready In: 2 hours 30 minutes

"Perfect for the Thanksgiving holiday, yams and apples are baked with a sweet glaze."

INGREDIENTS

4 large yams

3 tablespoons butter

1 tablespoon cornstarch

$1/2$ cup packed brown sugar

$1 1/2$ cups apple juice

1 tablespoon lemon juice

$1/2$ teaspoon ground cinnamon

$1/2$ teaspoon ground allspice

3 large apples - peeled, cored and sliced

DIRECTIONS

1. Place yams in a large saucepan with enough water to cover. Bring to a boil, and cook 30 minutes, or until tender but firm. Drain, peel, and cut into $1/3$ inch thick slices.

2. Preheat oven to 375°F (190°C). Lightly grease a 9x13 inch baking dish.

3. In a small saucepan over medium heat, melt the butter with the cornstarch and brown sugar. Mix in the apple juice, lemon juice, cinnamon, and allspice.

4. Alternate layers of yams and apples in the prepared baking dish. Pour the apple juice mixture over the layers.

5. Cover, and bake 1 hour in the preheated oven. Remove cover, and continue baking 30 minutes. Baste frequently with the juices from the pan to prevent drying.

Butternut Squash with Onions and Pecans

Submitted by: **Chris Lipo**

Makes: 8 servings

Preparation: 20 minutes

Cooking: 40 minutes

Ready In: 1 hour

"A new twist on a squash dish! The vegetables can be made 4 hours ahead, just reheat, stir in the pecans, and serve."

INGREDIENTS

1 cup chopped pecans

3 tablespoons butter

1 large onion, finely chopped

2¹/₄ pounds butternut squash - peeled, seeded, and cubed

salt and pepper to taste

3 tablespoons chopped fresh parsley

DIRECTIONS

1. Place pecans on an ungreased baking sheet. Toast at 350°F (175°C) for 5 to 8 minutes.

2. Melt butter in a large, heavy skillet over low heat; add onion, and saute until very tender, about 15 minutes. Stir in squash, and cover. Continue cooking, stirring occasionally, until squash is tender but still holds its shape, about 15 minutes. Season with salt and pepper.

3. Stir in half the pecans and half the parsley. Transfer mixture to a serving bowl. Sprinkle with remaining pecans and parsley to serve.

Squash Casserole

Submitted by: **Gayle A. Cox**

Makes: 8 servings

Preparation: 15 minutes

Cooking: 55 minutes

Ready In: 1 hour 10 minutes

"This casserole makes a rich, creamy vegetable side dish. Stuffing mix may be used in place of the bread crumbs if you prefer. It tastes even better the next day for leftovers."

INGREDIENTS

2 pounds crookneck yellow squash, sliced

1 small onion, chopped

1 (10.75 ounce) can condensed cream of chicken soup

1 (8 ounce) container sour cream

1/4 cup butter, melted

1 1/2 cups bread crumbs

DIRECTIONS

1. Preheat the oven to 350°F (175°C).

2. Place the squash and onion in a large saucepan with just enough water to cover. Bring to a boil over medium heat, and cook until tender, about 10 minutes.

3. Transfer the squash, onion, and remaining liquid from the saucepan to a 2½ quart casserole dish. Stir in chicken soup, sour cream, and melted butter. The liquid from the cooked squash should be enough so that mixture is slightly soupy. Sprinkle the bread crumbs over the top. The bread will absorb some of the liquid.

4. Bake, uncovered, for 30 to 45 minutes in the preheated oven, until browned and bubbly.

Baked Stuffed Pumpkin

Submitted by: **Debbi Raffalli**

Makes: 6 servings

Preparation: 30 minutes

Cooking: 1 hour

Ready In: 1 hour 30 minutes

"This recipe is wonderful as a side dish, and it is very impressive when you bring the whole pumpkin to the table! May be served spooned over pound cake or pumpkin bread, and garnished with whipped cream."

INGREDIENTS

1 medium sugar pumpkin

6 Granny Smith apples - peeled, cored and chopped

1 cup chopped walnuts

1 (16 ounce) can whole berry cranberry sauce

1 (20 ounce) can pineapple chunks, drained

3/4 cup packed brown sugar

1/2 cup golden raisins

1/2 cup dark rum (optional)

2 teaspoons minced fresh ginger root

1 tablespoon freshly grated nutmeg

1 tablespoon ground cinnamon

DIRECTIONS

1. Preheat oven to 350°F (175°C). Position rack in the center of the oven.

2. Cut out top of pumpkin, and set aside. Scoop out seeds with a metal spoon.

3. In a large bowl, stir together the apples, walnuts, cranberry sauce, pineapple, brown sugar, raisins, and rum. Season with ginger, nutmeg, and cinnamon, and mix well. Spoon the mixture into the cleaned pumpkin, and replace top.

4. Set pumpkin directly on a baking stone or a thick baking sheet. Bake for 1 hour in the preheated oven, or until pumpkin begins to soften. Remove from heat, and stir, scraping the sides gently, so that some pieces of pumpkin fall into the apple mixture.

Roasted Vegetables

Submitted by: **Saundra**

Makes: 12 servings

Preparation: 15 minutes

Cooking: 40 minutes

Ready In: 55 minutes

"A casserole dish of seasonal vegetables that is so easy to prepare. It can be made a day ahead - just reheat before serving. Lemon juice can be substituted for balsamic vinegar, and you can use baking potatoes if you don't have any Yukon Golds on hand."

INGREDIENTS

1 small butternut squash, cubed

2 red bell peppers, seeded and diced

1 sweet potato, peeled and cubed

3 Yukon Gold potatoes, cubed

1 red onion, quartered

1 tablespoon chopped fresh thyme

2 tablespoons chopped fresh rosemary

1/4 cup olive oil

2 tablespoons balsamic vinegar

salt and freshly ground black pepper

DIRECTIONS

1. Preheat oven to 475°F (245°C).

2. In a large bowl, combine the squash, red bell peppers, sweet potato, and Yukon Gold potatoes. Separate the red onion quarters into pieces, and add them to the mixture.

3. In a small bowl, stir together thyme, rosemary, olive oil, vinegar, salt, and pepper. Toss with vegetables until they are coated. Spread evenly on a large roasting pan.

4. Roast for 35 to 40 minutes in the preheated oven, stirring every 10 minutes, or until vegetables are cooked through and browned.

Favorite Green Bean Casserole

Submitted by: **Christine**

Makes: 8 servings

Preparation: 15 minutes

Cooking: 45 minutes

Ready In: 1 hour

"Frozen green beans, colorful pimentos and French-fried onions are baked to tender perfection in this wonderful, easy to make casserole."

INGREDIENTS

2 (16 ounce) packages frozen cut green beans

1 cup water

1 (10.75 ounce) can condensed cream of mushroom soup

1/2 cup milk

1 (4 ounce) jar diced pimento peppers, drained

1/8 teaspoon ground black pepper

1 (2.8 ounce) can French-fried onions

DIRECTIONS

1. Preheat oven to 350°F (175°C).

2. In a medium saucepan over medium heat, place the green beans in water, and bring to a boil. Cover, and cook 6 minutes, until tender. Remove from heat, and drain.

3. In an 8x8 inch baking dish, mix together the cream of mushroom soup, milk, pimentos, and pepper. Stir in the green beans. Sprinkle with French-fried onions.

4. Bake, uncovered, 30 to 40 minutes in the preheated oven, until the casserole is hot and bubbly in the center.

Lemon Pepper Green Beans

Submitted by: **Annette Byrdy**

Makes: 6 servings

Preparation: 5 minutes

Cooking: 20 minutes

Ready In: 25 minutes

"These green beans are easy and delicious. They are a bit tangy, spicy, and crunchy with the almonds. My family's favorite!"

INGREDIENTS

1 pound fresh green beans, rinsed and trimmed

2 tablespoons butter

1/4 cup sliced almonds

2 teaspoons lemon pepper

DIRECTIONS

1. Place green beans in a steamer over 1 inch of boiling water. Cover, and cook until tender but still firm, about 10 minutes; drain.

2. Meanwhile, melt butter in a skillet over medium heat. Saute almonds until lightly browned. Season with lemon pepper. Stir in green beans, and toss to coat.

Grandma's Green Bean Casserole

Submitted by: **Amy Barry**

Makes: 10 servings

Preparation: 15 minutes

Cooking: 40 minutes

Ready In: 55 minutes

"This recipe is much better than the standard mushroom soup and French fried onion version."

INGREDIENTS

2 tablespoons butter

2 tablespoons all-purpose flour

1 teaspoon salt

1 teaspoon white sugar

1/4 cup onion, diced

1 cup sour cream

3 (14.5 ounce) cans French style green beans, drained

2 cups shredded Cheddar cheese

1/2 cup crumbled buttery round crackers

1 tablespoon butter, melted

DIRECTIONS

1. Preheat oven to 350°F (175°C).

2. Melt 2 tablespoons butter in a large skillet over medium heat. Stir in flour until smooth, and cook for one minute. Stir in the salt, sugar, onion, and sour cream. Add green beans, and stir to coat.

3. Transfer the mixture to a 2½ quart casserole dish. Spread shredded cheese over the top. In a small bowl, toss together cracker crumbs and remaining butter, and sprinkle over the cheese.

4. Bake for 30 minutes in the preheated oven, or until the top is golden and cheese is bubbly.

Cheesy Green Beans

Submitted by: **Anna Marie**

Makes: 10 servings

Preparation: 10 minutes

Cooking: 30 minutes

Ready In: 40 minutes

"Cheese and bacon liven up plain green beans. This dish can be served immediately after preparing, but I often refrigerate it overnight to let the flavors blend together, then reheat it in a 350 degrees F (175 degrees C) oven until heated through."

INGREDIENTS

10 slices bacon

2 (16 ounce) packages frozen cut green beans

1 cup water

1 pound sliced fresh mushrooms

3/4 cup chopped onion

3/4 teaspoon ground black pepper

1 (16 ounce) jar processed cheese sauce

DIRECTIONS

1. Place bacon in a large, deep skillet. Cook over medium-high heat until evenly brown. Drain, crumble, and set aside. Reserve ¼ cup of bacon drippings in the skillet.

2. Place green beans and water in a medium saucepan, and bring to a boil. Reduce heat, cover, and simmer 6 minutes, or until tender but crisp; drain.

3. Place mushrooms and onion into the skillet with the reserved bacon drippings. Cook and stir over medium-high heat for 10 minutes; drain. Reserving 2 tablespoons for topping, mix the crumbled bacon into the skillet. Stir in the green beans. Season with pepper, and transfer to a 2 quart baking dish.

4. Melt the cheese sauce in the microwave, and pour over the green bean mixture. Sprinkle with reserved bacon, and serve.

Brussels Sprouts in Mustard Sauce

Submitted by: **Marilyn**

Makes: 6 servings

Preparation: 10 minutes

Cooking: 20 minutes

Ready In: 30 minutes

"The Brussels sprouts are cooked in chicken broth and therefore do not have the bitter aftertaste they have when cooked in water. My children love this recipe."

INGREDIENTS

2 tablespoons cornstarch

1/4 cup water

1 (14.5 ounce) can chicken broth

1 pound Brussels sprouts

2 teaspoons prepared Dijon-style mustard

2 teaspoons lemon juice

DIRECTIONS

1. Dissolve cornstarch in 1/4 cup water, and set aside.

2. In a medium saucepan over medium heat, bring chicken broth to a boil. Add Brussels sprouts, and cook until tender. Strain, reserving chicken broth, and place Brussels sprouts in a warm serving dish.

3. Return chicken broth to stove, stir in mustard and lemon juice, and return to boil. Add cornstarch mixture. Cook and stir until thickened. Pour over Brussels sprouts to serve.

Aunt Millie's Broccoli Casserole

Submitted by: **Kaylee**

Makes: 10 servings

Preparation: 15 minutes

Cooking: 40 minutes

Ready In: 55 minutes

"This is a family favorite for holidays and get-togethers! This recipe has been passed down in our family for years because it's so cheesy and delicious!"

INGREDIENTS

4 heads fresh broccoli, chopped

1 1/2 cups shredded American cheese

1 (10.75 ounce) can condensed cream of mushroom soup

1 1/2 teaspoons salt

2 teaspoons ground black pepper

3 tablespoons butter

2 cups crushed, seasoned croutons

DIRECTIONS

1. Preheat oven to 350°F (175°C).

2. Bring a pot of lightly salted water to a boil. Cook broccoli in the boiling water for 1 minute. Drain, and set aside.

3. In a saucepan over medium heat, mix the cheese, cream of mushroom soup, salt, and pepper. Stir until cheese is melted. Add the broccoli, stirring to coat. Transfer the mixture to a 9x13 inch baking dish.

4. In a separate saucepan, melt the butter over medium heat. Mix in the croutons, and sprinkle over the broccoli mixture.

5. Bake 30 minutes in the preheated oven, until the topping is browned and broccoli is tender.

Carrot Souffle

Submitted by: **Carol**

Makes: 8 servings

Preparation: 15 minutes

Cooking: 1 hour 15 minutes

Ready In: 1 hour 30 minutes

"A carrot souffle as good as your favorite restaurant makes!"

INGREDIENTS

1³/4 pounds carrots, peeled and chopped

1 cup white sugar

1¹/2 teaspoons baking powder

1¹/2 teaspoons vanilla extract

2 tablespoons all-purpose flour

3 eggs, beaten

¹/2 cup margarine, softened

2 teaspoons confectioners' sugar

DIRECTIONS

1. Preheat oven to 350°F (175°C).

2. In a large pot of boiling water, cook the carrots until very tender. Drain, and transfer to a large mixing bowl.

3. While carrots are warm, use an electric mixer to beat with sugar, baking powder, and vanilla extract until smooth. Mix in the flour, eggs, and margarine. Transfer to a 2 quart baking dish.

4. Bake 1 hour in the preheated oven, or until top is golden brown. Sprinkle lightly with confectioners' sugar before serving.

Corn Casserole

Submitted by: **Missy Borrowman**

Makes: 6 servings

Preparation: 10 minutes

Cooking: 1 hour

Ready In: 1 hour 10 minutes

"A creamy and slightly sweet corn and macaroni casserole. It always goes over with a big bang with family and friends."

INGREDIENTS

1 (15.25 ounce) can whole kernel corn, with liquid

1 (14.75 ounce) can cream style corn

1 cup small uncooked seashell pasta

1/2 cup butter, cut into pieces

1 cup cubed processed cheese

DIRECTIONS

1. Preheat oven to 350°F (175°C).

2. In a medium baking dish, mix the whole kernel corn, cream style corn, uncooked pasta, butter, and processed cheese.

3. Bake, covered, for 30 minutes in the preheated oven. Remove cover, stir, and continue baking 30 minutes, or until the pasta is tender but firm.

Corn Pudding V

Submitted by: **Becky**

Makes: 12 servings

Preparation: 15 minutes

Cooking: 45 minutes

Ready In: 1 hour

"This has become a family favorite, and a favorite at church pot-lucks. The best thing is how simple it is!"

INGREDIENTS

1 (15.25 ounce) can whole kernel corn, drained

1 (15 ounce) can cream style corn

¹/₂ cup margarine, softened

1 cup sour cream

1 (8.5 ounce) package dry cornbread mix

DIRECTIONS

1.   Preheat oven to 350°F (175°C). Lightly grease a 2 quart casserole dish.

2.   In a medium bowl, mix together the whole kernel corn, cream style corn, margarine, sour cream, and corn bread mix. Pour into the prepared casserole dish.

3.   Bake for 45 minutes in the preheated oven, or until a knife inserted in the center comes out clean.

Cranberry Sauce

Submitted by: **Toni**

Makes: 12 servings

Preparation: 5 minutes

Cooking: 10 minutes

Ready In: 15 minutes

"The tart flavor of cranberries makes a nice complement to any Holiday feast. This is a classic!"

INGREDIENTS

1 cup white sugar

1 cup orange juice

1 (12 ounce) package fresh cranberries

DIRECTIONS

1. In a medium saucepan over medium heat, dissolve the sugar in the orange juice. Stir in the cranberries, and cook until they start to pop (about 10 minutes). Remove from heat, and transfer to a bowl. Cranberry sauce will thicken as it cools.

Oranged Cranberry Sauce

Submitted by: **Barbara Yoder**

Makes: 24 servings

Preparation: 10 minutes

Cooking: 1 hour 15 minutes

Ready In: 1 hour 25 minutes

"This recipe was graciously shared with me by a Jamaican friend many years ago. It makes a delicious sauce, different from any other cranberry sauce I've ever tasted or made. It does not 'gel,' but you do want to cook it long enough to make a good, thick consistency."

INGREDIENTS

2 (12 ounce) packages fresh cranberries

1 orange, zested

3 cinnamon sticks

2 cups orange juice

2 cups packed brown sugar

DIRECTIONS

1. In a medium saucepan, combine cranberries, orange zest, cinnamon, orange juice, and brown sugar. Add enough water to cover, and bring to a boil over high heat. Immediately reduce heat, and simmer for about 1 hour, or until the sauce has thickened. Taste for sweetness, and adjust with additional sugar if necessary. You can not overcook, so continue cooking until you have a good thick consistency. Let mixture cool, then refrigerate in a covered container.

Cranberry Sauce Extraordinaire

Submitted by: **Leeza**

Makes: 12 servings

Preparation: 10 minutes

Cooking: 35 minutes

Ready In: 45 minutes

"This has been a 'trade secret' for years, but it's so good I decided to share it! It's everyone's favorite, and can even be poured over a block of cream cheese and served with crackers for a fun holiday appetizer."

INGREDIENTS

1 cup water

1 cup white sugar

1 (12 ounce) package fresh cranberries

1 orange, peeled and pureed

1 apple - peeled, cored and diced

1 pear - peeled, cored and diced

1 cup chopped dried mixed fruit

1 cup chopped pecans

$1/2$ teaspoon salt

1 teaspoon ground cinnamon

$1/2$ teaspoon ground nutmeg

DIRECTIONS

1. In a medium saucepan, boil water and sugar until the sugar dissolves. Reduce the heat to simmer, and stir in cranberries, pureed orange, apple, pear, dried fruit, pecans, salt, cinnamon, and nutmeg. Cover, and simmer for 30 minutes, stirring occasionally, until the cranberries burst. Remove from heat, and let cool to room temperature.

Baked Cranberry Sauce

Submitted by: **Marion**

Makes: 16 servings

Preparation: 5 minutes

Cooking: 1 hour

Ready In: 1 hour 5 minutes

"This brandy baked cranberry sauce is simply delicious."

INGREDIENTS

4 cups fresh cranberries

2 cups white sugar

1/3 cup brandy

DIRECTIONS

1. Preheat oven to 300°F (150°C).

2. In a baking dish, mix the cranberries and sugar.

3. Bake 1 hour in the preheated oven, stirring often. Mix in the brandy to serve.

Apricot/Cranberry Chutney

Submitted by: **Sher**

Makes: 12 servings

Preparation: 10 minutes

Cooking: 15 minutes

Ready In: 30 minutes

"A terrific recipe that my mother-in-law gave me. We have enjoyed it as an alternative to the traditional cranberry sauce! She doesn't mind sharing it!"

INGREDIENTS

1/4 cup diced dried apricots

1 (12 ounce) package fresh cranberries

1/2 cup raisins

3/4 teaspoon ground cinnamon

1/4 teaspoon ground ginger

1/4 teaspoon ground allspice

1 pinch ground cloves

1 cup water

3/4 cup white sugar

1/2 cup cider vinegar

DIRECTIONS

1. In a medium bowl, mix together the apricots, cranberries, raisins, cinnamon, ginger, allspice, and cloves.

2. In a medium saucepan, boil water and sugar, stirring constantly, until sugar is dissolved. Add the dried fruit mixture and vinegar. Bring to a boil, reduce heat, and simmer for 10 minutes. Remove from heat, and allow to cool for 5 minutes. Serve immediately, or refrigerate in a covered container.

Harvest Rice Dish

Submitted by: **Kathy Alexander**

Makes: 6 servings

Preparation: 15 minutes

Cooking: 1 hour 30 minutes

Ready In: 1 hour 45 minutes

"A variation of a basic rice recipe for the holidays."

INGREDIENTS

1/2 cup slivered almonds

2 cups chicken broth

1/2 cup uncooked brown rice

1/2 cup uncooked wild rice

3 tablespoons butter

3 onions, sliced into 1/2 inch wedges

1 tablespoon brown sugar

1 cup dried cranberries

2/3 cup fresh sliced mushrooms

1/2 teaspoon orange zest

salt and pepper to taste

DIRECTIONS

1. Place almonds on an ungreased baking sheet. Toast at 350°F (175°C) for 5 to 8 minutes.

2. Mix broth, brown rice, and wild rice in a medium saucepan, and bring to boil. Reduce heat to low, cover, and simmer 45 minutes, until rice is tender and broth is absorbed.

3. In medium skillet, melt butter over medium-high heat. Add onions and brown sugar. Saute until butter is absorbed and onions are translucent and soft. Reduce heat, and cook onions for another 20 minutes, until they are caramelized.

4. Stir cranberries and mushrooms into the skillet. Cover, and cook 10 minutes or until berries start to swell. Stir in almonds and orange zest, then fold the mixture into the cooked rice. Salt and pepper to taste.

Carrots and Rice

Submitted by: **Gayle Frazier**

Makes: 12 servings

Preparation: 15 minutes

Cooking: 40 minutes

Ready In: 55 minutes

"Creamy rice and sweet, buttery carrots go with just about any meal. This recipe was a specialty of my mother's. It has been served in our family for Thanksgiving and Christmas for over 25 years, but it can be served anytime. It is very rich and quite delish."

INGREDIENTS

1 cup sliced carrots

3 tablespoons minced onion

4 1/2 cups water

2 teaspoons salt

2 cups uncooked long grain white rice

1/2 cup white sugar

1 cup half-and-half cream

3/4 cup butter

DIRECTIONS

1. In a large saucepan, combine carrots, onion, water, and salt. Bring to a boil, reduce heat to medium, and simmer for 10 minutes. Stir in rice. Reduce heat to low, and cover pan. Allow to steam for 20 minutes.

2. Stir sugar, half-and-half, and butter into rice mixture. Consistency should be creamy, not dry. Stir in some milk if necessary. Remove from heat, and serve immediately.

Savory Turkey Gravy

Submitted by: **Veronica Harper**

Makes: 6 cups

Preparation: 5 minutes

Cooking: 15 minutes

Ready In: 20 minutes

"Everyone just loves this tasty gravy. It's a favorite among my family and friends."

INGREDIENTS

5 cups turkey stock

1/4 cup all-purpose flour

1 cup water

1 teaspoon poultry seasoning

1 teaspoon salt

1/2 teaspoon ground black pepper

1/4 teaspoon celery salt

DIRECTIONS

1. In a medium saucepan, bring the turkey stock to a boil. In a small bowl, dissolve flour in water. Gradually whisk into the turkey stock. Season with poultry seasoning, salt, pepper, and celery salt. Bring to a boil, reduce heat, and simmer for 8 to 10 minutes, or until thickened.

Vegetarian Gravy

Submitted by: **Becky**

Makes: 2¹/₂ cups

Preparation: 10 minutes

Cooking: 20 minutes

Ready In: 30 minutes

"This is a delicious vegetarian gravy!"

INGREDIENTS

¹/₂ cup vegetable oil

¹/₃ cup chopped onion

5 cloves garlic, minced

¹/₂ cup all-purpose flour

4 teaspoons nutritional yeast

4 tablespoons light soy sauce

2 cups vegetable broth

¹/₂ teaspoon dried sage

¹/₂ teaspoon salt

¹/₄ teaspoon ground black pepper

DIRECTIONS

1. Heat oil in a medium saucepan over medium heat. Saute onion and garlic until soft and translucent, about 5 minutes. Stir in flour, nutritional yeast, and soy sauce to form a smooth paste. Gradually whisk in the broth. Season with sage, salt, and pepper. Bring to a boil. Reduce heat, and simmer, stirring constantly, for 8 to 10 minutes, or until thickened.

Cranberry Waldorf

Submitted by: **Thea**

Makes: 12 servings

Preparation: 15 minutes

Ready In: 2 hours 15 minutes

"I make this salad all year long, but it is especially great for Thanksgiving and Christmas. Just freeze a few bags of cranberries to use at a later date. I know this will become a tradition to anyone who tries it, it's delicious! Garnish with frosted cranberries and mint leaves, if desired. For frosted cranberries, wet cranberries with water, and roll in sugar."

INGREDIENTS

1 1/2 cups chopped cranberries

1 cup chopped red apple

1 cup chopped celery

1 cup seedless green grapes, halved

1/3 cup raisins

1/4 cup chopped walnuts

2 tablespoons white sugar

1/4 teaspoon ground cinnamon

1 (8 ounce) container vanilla low-fat yogurt

DIRECTIONS

1. In a medium bowl, combine cranberries, apple, celery, grapes, raisins, walnuts, sugar, cinnamon, and yogurt. (I chop cranberries in a food processor, and it works great). Toss to coat. Cover, and chill 2 hours. Stir just before serving.

Winter Fruit Salad with Lemon Poppyseed Dressing

Makes: 12 servings

Preparation: 25 minutes

Ready In: 25 minutes

Submitted by: **Nora LaCroix**

"Wonderful salad for the holiday seasons. Great to serve for dinner at home or to take to a family gathering during the holidays."

INGREDIENTS

1/2 cup white sugar

1/2 cup lemon juice

2 teaspoons diced onion

1 teaspoon Dijon-style prepared mustard

1/2 teaspoon salt

2/3 cup vegetable oil

1 tablespoon poppy seeds

1 head romaine lettuce, torn into bite-size pieces

4 ounces shredded Swiss cheese

1 cup cashews

1/4 cup dried cranberries

1 apple - peeled, cored and diced

1 pear - peeled, cored and sliced

DIRECTIONS

1. In a blender or food processor, combine sugar, lemon juice, onion, mustard, and salt. Process until well blended. With machine still running, add oil in a slow, steady stream until mixture is thick and smooth. Add poppy seeds, and process just a few seconds more to mix.

2. In a large serving bowl, toss together the romaine lettuce, shredded Swiss cheese, cashews, dried cranberries, apple, and pear. Pour dressing over salad just before serving, and toss to coat.

desserts

Give all of your holiday celebrations a happy ending with an unforgettable dessert. From the simple traditions, like pumpkin pie, to the more elaborate cake-baking that takes center stage, amaze your guests with these favorite holiday desserts. There will always be room for one more bite.

Santa's Favorite Cake

Submitted by: **Debbie Rowe**

Makes: 1 - 3 layer cake

Preparation: 45 minutes

Cooking: 25 minutes

Ready In: 2 hours 10 minutes

"This cake is a red velvet cake with a peppermint twist, and a delicious pepper-mint cream cheese frosting."

INGREDIENTS

1 (18.25 ounce) package white cake mix

3 egg whites

1 1/3 cups buttermilk

2 tablespoons vegetable oil

1 (9 ounce) package yellow cake mix

1/2 cup buttermilk

1 egg

1 1/2 tablespoons unsweetened cocoa powder

2 tablespoons red food coloring

1 teaspoon cider vinegar

1 (8 ounce) package cream cheese, softened

1 cup margarine, softened

2 (16 ounce) packages confectioners' sugar

2 teaspoons peppermint extract

DIRECTIONS

1. Preheat oven to 350°F (175°C). Grease and flour three 9 inch round cake pans.

2. In a large bowl, combine white cake mix, 3 egg whites, 1⅓ cups buttermilk, and 2 tablespoons vegetable oil. Mix with an electric mixer for 2 minutes on high speed. In a separate bowl, combine yellow cake mix, ½ cup buttermilk, 1 egg, cocoa, red food coloring, and vinegar. Use an electric mixer to beat for 2 minutes on high speed.

3. Spoon white batter alternately with red batter into the prepared cake pans. Swirl batter gently with a knife to create a marbled effect.

4. Bake in preheated oven for 22 to 25 minutes, or until a wooden pick inserted into the centers comes out clean. Let cool in pans for at least 10 minutes before turning out onto a wire rack to cool completely.

5. In a large bowl, beat cream cheese and margarine until smooth. Gradually blend in sugar until incorporated and smooth. Stir in peppermint extract. Spread peppermint cream cheese frosting between layers, and on top and sides of cake.

Eggnog Cake

Submitted by: **Tony**

Makes: 1 - 8x4 inch loaf pan
Preparation: 20 minutes
Cooking: 1 hour 5 minutes
Ready In: 1 hour 25 minutes

"An eggnog flavored pound cake, wonderful for holiday gatherings."

INGREDIENTS

2 cups all-purpose flour

1 tablespoon baking powder

1 teaspoon salt

1 teaspoon ground nutmeg

1/4 teaspoon ground ginger

1 cup white sugar

1/4 cup butter

1/4 cup shortening

2 eggs

1 teaspoon rum flavored extract

3/4 cup milk

DIRECTIONS

1. Preheat oven to 350°F (175°C). Grease and flour an 8x4 inch loaf pan. Sift together the flour, baking powder, salt, nutmeg, and ginger; set aside.

2. In a large bowl, cream together sugar, butter, and shortening until light and fluffy. Blend in the eggs one at a time, then stir in the rum extract. Beat in the flour mixture alternately with the milk, mixing just until incorporated. Pour batter into prepared pan.

3. Bake in the preheated oven for 65 to 70 minutes, or until a toothpick inserted into the center of the cake comes out clean.

Chocolate Plum Pudding Cake

Submitted by: **Carol**

Makes: 1 - 9 inch tube cake

Preparation: 25 minutes

Cooking: 1 hour 20 minutes

Ready In: 1 hour 45 minutes

"This is a bit of an unusual cake, but great for Christmas. The chocolate mixed with raisins, applesauce, and spices gives a nice texture with a lot less work than plum pudding itself."

INGREDIENTS

- 2/3 cup raisins
- 3/4 cup all-purpose flour
- 3/4 cup whole wheat flour
- 1/3 cup unsweetened cocoa powder
- 2 teaspoons baking soda
- 1/4 teaspoon salt
- 1 tablespoon ground cinnamon
- 1/2 teaspoon ground nutmeg
- 3/4 cup butter, softened
- 1 1/2 cups white sugar
- 3 eggs
- 2 cups applesauce
- 1/2 cup coarsely chopped walnuts

DIRECTIONS

1. Preheat oven to 350°F (175°C). Place raisins in a small saucepan, and cover with boiling water. Soak for 5 minutes, then drain. Grease and flour a 9 inch tube pan.

2. Sift together the all-purpose flour, whole wheat flour, cocoa, baking soda, salt, cinnamon, and nutmeg. Set aside.

3. In a large bowl, cream butter and sugar until light and fluffy. Blend in the eggs, then the applesauce. Beat in the flour mixture. Stir in raisins and walnuts. Spread batter evenly into prepared tube pan.

4. Bake in preheated oven for 80 minutes, or until a toothpick inserted in the center of cake comes out clean. Let cool in pan for 10 minutes, then turn out onto a wire rack and cool completely; chill.

Buche de Noel

Submitted by: **Tyra**

Makes: 1 Buche de Noel

Preparation: 45 minutes

Cooking: 15 minutes

Ready In: 1 hour 30 minutes

"Buche de Noel is the French name for a Christmas cake shaped like a log. This one is a heavenly flourless chocolate cake rolled with chocolate whipped cream. Traditionally, Buche de Noel is decorated with confectioners' sugar to resemble snow on a Yule log."

INGREDIENTS

2 cups heavy cream

1/2 cup confectioners' sugar

1/2 cup unsweetened cocoa powder

1 teaspoon vanilla extract

6 egg yolks

1/2 cup white sugar

1/3 cup unsweetened cocoa powder

1 1/2 teaspoons vanilla extract

1/8 teaspoon salt

6 egg whites

1/4 cup white sugar

confectioners' sugar for dusting

DIRECTIONS

1. Preheat oven to 375 °F (190°C). Line a 10x15 inch jellyroll pan with parchment paper. In a large bowl, whip cream, 1/2 cup confectioners' sugar, 1/2 cup cocoa, and 1 teaspoon vanilla until thick and stiff. Refrigerate.

2. In a large bowl, use an electric mixer to beat egg yolks with 1/2 cup sugar until thick and pale. Blend in 1/3 cup cocoa, 1 1/2 teaspoons vanilla, and salt. In large glass bowl, using clean beaters, whip egg whites to soft peaks. Gradually add 1/4 cup sugar, and beat until whites form stiff peaks. Immediately fold the yolk mixture into the whites. Spread the batter evenly into the prepared pan.

3. Bake for 12 to 15 minutes in the preheated oven, or until the cake springs back when lightly touched. Dust a clean dishtowel with confectioners' sugar. Run a knife around the edge of the pan, and turn the warm cake out onto the towel. Remove and discard parchment paper. Starting at the short edge of the cake, roll the cake up with the towel. Cool for 30 minutes.

4. Unroll the cake, and spread the filling to within 1 inch of the edge. Roll the cake up with the filling inside. Place seam side down onto a serving plate, and refrigerate until serving. Dust with confectioners' sugar before serving.

Pumpkin Roll

Submitted by: **Tammy Elliott**

Makes: 1 pumpkin roll

Preparation: 35 minutes

Cooking: 20 minutes

Ready In: 25 hours 15 minutes

"This is a great dessert, especially nice for holidays, but it can be served anytime of the year. The resulting pumpkin roll slices will impress your guests. The pumpkin roll is not as hard to make as it sounds. Be sure and use plain canned pumpkin, and not pumpkin pie mix."

INGREDIENTS

3 eggs

1 cup white sugar

2/3 cup solid pack pumpkin puree

1 teaspoon lemon juice

3/4 cup all-purpose flour

1 teaspoon baking powder

1/2 teaspoon salt

2 teaspoons ground cinnamon

1 teaspoon ground ginger

1 cup chopped pecans

confectioners' sugar for dusting

1 (8 ounce) package cream cheese

4 tablespoons butter

1 cup confectioners' sugar

1/2 teaspoon vanilla extract

confectioners' sugar for dusting

DIRECTIONS

1. Preheat oven to 350°F (175°C). Grease and flour a 10x15 inch jellyroll pan.

2. In a large bowl, beat eggs and sugar with an electric mixer on high speed for five minutes. Gradually mix in pumpkin and lemon juice. Combine the flour, baking powder, salt, cinnamon, and ginger; stir into the pumpkin mixture. Spread batter evenly into the prepared pan. Sprinkle pecans over the top of the batter.

3. Bake for 12 to 15 minutes, or until the center springs back when touched. Loosen edges with a knife. Turn out on two dishtowels that have been dusted with confectioners' sugar. Roll up cake using towels, and let cool for about 20 minutes.

4. In a medium bowl, combine cream cheese, butter, 1 cup confectioners' sugar, and vanilla. Beat until smooth. Unroll pumpkin cake when cool, spread with filling, and roll up. Place pumpkin roll on a long sheet of waxed paper, and dust with confectioners' sugar. Wrap cake in waxed paper, and twist ends of waxed paper like a candy wrapper. Refrigerate overnight. Serve chilled; before slicing, dust with additional confectioners' sugar.

Marbled Pumpkin Cheesecake

Submitted by: **Renee**

Makes: 1 - 9 inch cake

Preparation: 30 minutes

Cooking: 1 hour 10 minutes

Ready In: 7 hours 40 minutes

"This is a wonderful pumpkin cheesecake with a gingersnap crust. The ginger-snap really does make a difference."

INGREDIENTS

1 1/2 cups crushed gingersnap cookies

1/2 cup finely chopped pecans

1/3 cup butter, melted

2 (8 ounce) packages cream cheese, softened

3/4 cup white sugar, divided

1 teaspoon vanilla extract

3 eggs

1 cup canned pumpkin

3/4 teaspoon ground cinnamon

1/4 teaspoon ground nutmeg

DIRECTIONS

1. Preheat oven to 350°F (175°C). In a medium bowl, mix together the crushed gingersnap cookies, pecans, and butter. Press into the bottom, and about 1 inch up the sides of a 9 inch springform pan. Bake crust 10 minutes in the preheated oven. Set aside to cool.

2. In a medium bowl, mix together the cream cheese, ½ cup sugar, and vanilla just until smooth. Mix in eggs one at a time, blending well after each. Set aside 1 cup of the mixture. Blend ¼ cup sugar, pumpkin, cinnamon, and nutmeg into the remaining mixture.

3. Spread the pumpkin flavored batter into the crust, and drop the plain batter by spoonfuls onto the top. Swirl with a knife to create a marbled effect.

4. Bake 55 minutes in the preheated oven, or until filling is set. Run a knife around the edge of the pan. Allow to cool before removing pan rim. Chill for at least 4 hours before serving.

Eggnog Cheesecake

Submitted by: **Eleanor Johnson**

Makes: 1 - 9 inch cheesecake

Preparation: 40 minutes

Cooking: 1 hour 10 minutes

Ready In: 6 hours

"A simple easy-to-make cheesecake served with a yummy Pecan Caramel Sauce. It's perfect for holiday get-togethers."

INGREDIENTS

¼ cup butter, melted

1¼ cups vanilla wafer crumbs

¼ cup white sugar

3 (8 ounce) packages cream cheese, softened

1 (14 ounce) can sweetened condensed milk

3 eggs

¼ cup dark rum

1 teaspoon vanilla extract

½ teaspoon ground nutmeg

1 tablespoon cornstarch

1 cup water

2 tablespoons butter, melted

⅓ cup packed light brown sugar

2 tablespoons dark rum

½ cup chopped pecans

DIRECTIONS

1. Preheat oven to 300°F (150°C).

2. In a large bowl, combine ¼ cup butter, wafer crumbs, and white sugar. Press firmly on the bottom of a 9 inch springform pan.

3. In a large bowl, beat the cream cheese until fluffy. Gradually beat in the sweetened condensed milk until smooth. Mix in the eggs. Stir in ¼ cup rum, vanilla extract, and nutmeg. Pour into the prepared pan.

4. Bake in preheated oven for 40 to 50 minutes, or until center of cake springs back when lightly touched. Allow to cool, then chill.

5. To Make The Pecan Caramel Sauce: In a small bowl, dissolve the cornstarch in 1 cup of water. In a medium saucepan, melt 2 tablespoons butter. Stir in brown sugar and the cornstarch mixture. Bring to a boil, stirring constantly. Reduce heat, and simmer for 10 minutes. Remove from heat, and add 2 tablespoons dark rum. Allow to cool. Just before serving, stir the pecans into the sauce.

6. Remove the sides of the springform pan from the cooled cheesecake. Serve with the Pecan Caramel Sauce.

White Chocolate Raspberry Cheesecake

Submitted by: **Cindy**

Makes: 1 - 9 inch cheesecake

Preparation: 1 hour

Cooking: 1 hour

Ready In: 10 hours

"This makes an excellent cheesecake, similar to one you would get in a restaurant. Great for special occasions! Garnish with white chocolate curls if desired."

INGREDIENTS

1 cup chocolate cookie crumbs

3 tablespoons white sugar

1/4 cup butter, melted

1 (10 ounce) package frozen raspberries

2 tablespoons white sugar

2 teaspoons cornstarch

1/2 cup water

2 cups white chocolate chips

1/2 cup half-and-half cream

3 (8 ounce) packages cream cheese, softened

1/2 cup white sugar

3 eggs

1 teaspoon vanilla extract

DIRECTIONS

1. In a medium bowl, mix together cookie crumbs, 3 tablespoons sugar, and melted butter. Press mixture into the bottom of a 9 inch springform pan.

2. In a saucepan, combine raspberries, 2 tablespoons sugar, cornstarch, and water. Bring to boil, and continue boiling 5 minutes, or until sauce is thick. Strain sauce through a mesh strainer to remove seeds.

3. Preheat oven to 325°F (165°C). In a metal bowl over a pan of simmering water, melt white chocolate chips with half-and-half, stirring occasionally until smooth.

4. In a large bowl, mix together cream cheese and ½ cup sugar until smooth. Beat in eggs one at a time. Blend in vanilla and melted white chocolate. Pour half of batter over crust. Spoon 3 tablespoons raspberry sauce over batter. Pour remaining cheesecake batter into pan, and again spoon 3 tablespoons raspberry sauce over the top. Swirl batter with the tip of a knife to create a marbled effect.

5. Bake for 55 to 60 minutes, or until filling is set. Cool, cover with plastic wrap, and refrigerate for 8 hours before removing from pan. Serve with remaining raspberry sauce.

Pie Crust

Submitted by: **Brenda**

Makes: 2 crusts

Preparation: 20 minutes

Ready In: 20 minutes

"This recipe can be halved to make one crust. Note: use 3 - 4 tablespoons of cold water when making only one crust."

INGREDIENTS

2 cups all-purpose flour

1 teaspoon salt

²/₃ cup shortening

6 tablespoons cold water

DIRECTIONS

1. Mix flour and salt in a large bowl. Cut in shortening with a pastry blender until mixture is completely blended and appears crumbly.

2. Mix in water, 1 tablespoon at a time, by lightly tossing with a fork. Add only enough water to form mixture into a ball. The dough will be sticky and tough if to much water is added, and it will crack and tear when rolled if too little is added.

3. Divide the dough into 2 balls, and roll each out into a circle 1 inch larger than the inverted pie plate.

4. Follow these directions for a filled pie: Fold one circle of dough in half, and gently lift. Place into pie plate, and unfold. Add filling to pie plate. Fold second circle of dough in half. Gently place over filling, and unfold. With a table knife, cut off excess crust evenly so that ½ to 1 inch extends beyond the edge of the pie plate. Fold under the excess dough so that it is even with the edge of the pie plate. Flute the edge of the crust. Cut slits in top crust for steam to escape.

5. Follow these directions for 2 prebaked pie shells: Fold circle of dough in half, and gently lift. Place into pie plate, and unfold. Either prick the entire surface of dough with a fork, or weight the bottom of the crust with pie weights while baking. Pie weights can be uncooked rice, dried beans, small clean pebbles, or small balls sold as pie weights.

Brown Family's Favorite Pumpkin Pie

Submitted by: **Cindy B.**

Makes: 1 - 9 inch pie

Preparation: 30 minutes

Cooking: 1 hour

Ready In: 1 hour 30 minutes

"This pumpkin pie has a walnut, streusel topping that is optional. Serve with whipped topping or ice cream."

INGREDIENTS

1 (15 ounce) can pumpkin puree

1 (14 ounce) can sweetened condensed milk

2 egg yolks

1 teaspoon ground cinnamon

1/2 teaspoon ground ginger

1/2 teaspoon ground nutmeg

1/2 teaspoon salt

2 egg whites

1 (9 inch) unbaked pie shell

2 tablespoons all-purpose flour

1/4 cup packed brown sugar

1 teaspoon ground cinnamon

2 tablespoons butter, chilled

1 cup chopped walnuts

DIRECTIONS

1. Preheat the oven to 425°F (220°C).

2. In a large bowl, mix together the pumpkin, sweetened condensed milk, and egg yolks. Stir in 1 teaspoon cinnamon, ginger, nutmeg, and salt. In a large glass or metal bowl, whip egg whites until soft peaks form. Gently fold into pumpkin mixture. Pour filling into pie shell.

3. Bake for 15 minutes in the preheated oven. While the pie is baking, prepare the streusel topping: In a small bowl, combine the flour, brown sugar, and 1 teaspoon cinnamon. Blend in the cold butter with a fork or pastry blender until the mixture is crumbly. Mix in the chopped nuts. Sprinkle the topping over the pie.

4. Reduce the heat to 350°F (175°C). Bake an additional 40 minutes, or until set.

Cindy's Pumpkin Pie

Submitted by: **Cindy**

Makes: 2 - 9 inch pies

Preparation: 15 minutes

Cooking: 45 minutes

Ready In: 1 hour

"This pumpkin pie recipe uses melted ice cream instead of evaporated milk. The result is delicious. I have never brought home leftovers of this pie. I recommend using fresh pumpkin, but canned pumpkin can also be used."

INGREDIENTS

1 1/2 pints vanilla ice cream, softened

3 eggs

1 3/4 cups pumpkin puree

3/4 cup white sugar

1/2 teaspoon salt

1 teaspoon ground cinnamon

1/4 teaspoon ground ginger

1/4 teaspoon ground nutmeg

2 (9 inch) unbaked pie shells

DIRECTIONS

1. Preheat oven to 425°F (220°C.) Place ice cream near the warm oven to soften.

2. In a large bowl, whisk together the eggs. Stir in the pumpkin puree, sugar, salt, cinnamon, ginger, and nutmeg. Mix in soft ice cream until smooth. Pour filling into two 9 inch pie shells.

3. Bake for 15 minutes in the preheated oven. Reduce temperature to 350°F (175°C), and bake an additional 30 to 40 minutes, or until filling is set.

Pumpkin Maple Pie Supreme

Submitted by: **Carole Rhodus**

Makes: 1 - 9 inch pie

Preparation: 30 minutes

Cooking: 2 hours

Ready In: 2 hours 30 minutes

"The first pumpkin pies were nothing like we make today. The most available sweetener was maple syrup, REAL maple syrup. I decided to try adding that to these pies and what a difference! This is my husband's favorite pie, using actual pumpkins that we grow. Using REAL maple syrup is key to the flavor. For extra special times, I serve with maple-sweetened whipped cream."

INGREDIENTS

1 small sugar pumpkin

3/4 cup packed brown sugar

1 1/4 teaspoons ground cinnamon

1 teaspoon ground ginger

1 teaspoon ground nutmeg

1/4 teaspoon ground cloves

1/8 teaspoon ground allspice

1/2 teaspoon salt

2/3 cup real maple syrup

1 1/4 cups half-and-half cream

1 teaspoon all-purpose flour

3 eggs

1 (9 inch) unbaked pie shell

DIRECTIONS

1. Preheat oven to 375°F (190°C)

2. Cut up pumpkin, and remove seeds. Place in large baking pan, and cover with foil or lid. Bake for 1 hour, or until very tender. Remove from oven, and set aside to cool. Reduce oven temperature to 350°F (175°C).

3. Scrape pumpkin into a food processor; puree until smooth. Measure 1½ cups pumpkin puree. In a large bowl, mix together 1½ cups pumpkin, brown sugar, cinnamon, ginger, nutmeg, cloves, allspice, and salt. Stir in maple syrup, half-and-half, and flour. Mix in eggs one at a time. Pour filling into unbaked pie shell.

4. Bake at 350°F (175°C) for 1 hour, or until center is set.

Better Than Pumpkin Pie

Submitted by: **Barbara**

Makes: 1 - 9 inch pie

Preparation: 20 minutes

Cooking: 50 minutes

Ready In: 1 hour 10 minutes

"Looks like pumpkin, tastes like pumpkin, but it's butternut squash!"

INGREDIENTS

1¹/₂ cups peeled and cubed butternut squash

1 cup lightly packed brown sugar

1 tablespoon cornstarch

1 egg, beaten

1 cup evaporated milk

1 teaspoon ground cinnamon

1 pinch ground allspice

1 pinch ground cloves

1 pinch ground ginger

1 pinch ground nutmeg

1 (9 inch) unbaked pie shell

DIRECTIONS

1. Place squash in a saucepan with enough water to cover. Bring to a boil, and simmer over medium heat until tender, about 15 minutes. Drain, and cool.

2. Preheat oven to 350°F (175°C).

3. In a blender or food processor, combine butternut squash, brown sugar, cornstarch, egg, milk, cinnamon, allspice, cloves, ginger, and nutmeg. Process until smooth. Pour into the unbaked pie shell.

4. Bake in preheated oven for 50 minutes, or until a table knife comes out clean when inserted in the center.

Pecan Pie

Submitted by: **Linda Seay**

Makes: 1 - 9 inch pie

Preparation: 10 minutes

Cooking: 1 hour

Ready In: 1 hour 10 minutes

"This is a wonderfully rich, Southern pie recipe that is the best I've tried!"

INGREDIENTS

1³/₄ cups white sugar

¹/₄ cup dark corn syrup

¹/₄ cup butter

1 tablespoon cold water

2 teaspoons cornstarch

3 eggs

¹/₄ teaspoon salt

1 teaspoon vanilla extract

1¹/₄ cups chopped pecans

1 (9 inch) unbaked pie shell

DIRECTIONS

1. Preheat oven to 350°F (175°C).

2. In a medium saucepan, combine the sugar, corn syrup, butter, water, and cornstarch. Bring to a full boil, and remove from heat.

3. In a large bowl, beat eggs until frothy. Gradually beat in cooked syrup mixture. Stir in salt, vanilla, and pecans. Pour into pie shell.

4. Bake in preheated oven for 45 to 50 minutes, or until filling is set.

Glazed Apple Cream Pie

Submitted by: **Kathy**

Makes: 1 - 9 inch pie

Preparation: 15 minutes

Cooking: 45 minutes

Ready In: 3 hours

"A friend who NEVER bakes gave me this recipe recently. I think she's made this pie once a week for the past 6 weeks now! This one is great!"

INGREDIENTS

1/2 cup white sugar

1/2 cup milk

1/2 cup heavy cream

1/4 cup butter

2 tablespoons cornstarch

2 tablespoons milk

1 teaspoon vanilla extract

2 tart apples - peeled, cored and sliced

1 tablespoon all-purpose flour

1/4 teaspoon ground cinnamon

1 (15 ounce) package pastry for double-crust pie

1/2 cup confectioners' sugar

1 tablespoon milk

1/4 teaspoon vanilla extract

1 tablespoon butter, softened

DIRECTIONS

1. In a medium saucepan over medium heat, combine ½ cup sugar, ½ cup milk, ½ cup cream, and ¼ cup butter. Heat until butter is melted, stirring occasionally. In a small bowl, whisk together the cornstarch, 2 tablespoons milk, and vanilla; stir into saucepan. Cook until thickened, stirring constantly. Remove from heat, and set aside to cool slightly.

2. Preheat oven to 400°F (200°C). In a medium bowl, combine the apples, flour, and cinnamon. Mix well.

3. Line a 9 inch pie pan with pie dough. Pour thickened filling mixture into pastry-lined pie pan. Arrange apple mixture evenly over filling. Top with second crust, seal and flute the edges. Cut slits in top crust.

4. Bake for 30 to 40 minutes, or until crust is golden brown and apples are tender. Cool for at least 30 minutes.

5. In small bowl, combine confectioners' sugar, 1 tablespoon milk, ¼ teaspoon vanilla, and 1 tablespoon softened butter. Blend until smooth; pour evenly over warm pie. Refrigerate for AT LEAST 1½ hours before serving (longer is better).

Cranberry Apple Pie

Submitted by: **Blythe**

Makes: 1 - 9 inch pie
Preparation: 30 minutes
Cooking: 1 hour
Ready In: 1 hour 30 minutes

"Slightly tart, crunchy-textured pie with a divine streusel topping."

INGREDIENTS

1 (9 inch) deep dish pie crust

6 apples - peeled, cored and chopped

1 (12 ounce) package fresh cranberries, roughly chopped

1 1/2 cups white sugar

1/3 cup quick-cooking tapioca

1 1/2 cups all-purpose flour

3/4 cup packed brown sugar

1 teaspoon ground cinnamon

1/2 teaspoon salt

2/3 cup unsalted butter

1 egg, lightly beaten

DIRECTIONS

1. Preheat oven to 325°F (165°C). Invert pie shell over another pie pan of equal size. This will keep the crust from shrinking down into the pan. Bake in this position for 10 minutes, until partially baked. Turn right side up, and remove the extra pie pan from inside the crust.

2. In a large bowl, combine apples, cranberries, and sugar. Cover, and set aside for about 20 minutes. Mix in tapioca, and set aside for 15 to 20 minutes, until tapioca has absorbed fruit juice. Spread mixture into the partially baked pie shell.

3. In a medium bowl, combine flour, brown sugar, cinnamon, salt, and butter. Work mixture with fingertips until crumbly. Spread mixture over the apple-cranberry filling. Brush exposed pie shell with lightly beaten egg.

4. Place the pie on a cookie sheet to catch drips. Bake 45 to 60 minutes on the bottom rack of the preheated oven, or until apples are tender when tested with a wooden pick.

Cranberry Apple Pie III

Submitted by: **Carolyn**

Makes: 1 - 9 inch pie

Preparation: 30 minutes

Cooking: 45 minutes

Ready In: 1 hour 15 minutes

"A delicious twist to the traditional apple pie! Wonderful when served warm with vanilla ice cream."

INGREDIENTS

1¼ cups white sugar

¼ cup all-purpose flour

¼ teaspoon salt

2 cups cranberries

¼ cup maple syrup

5 apples - peeled, cored and sliced

½ cup chopped walnuts

1 (9 inch) unbaked pie shell

1 cup dry bread crumbs

¾ cup all-purpose flour

¼ cup packed brown sugar

¼ cup butter, melted

DIRECTIONS

1. Preheat oven to 375°F (190°C).

2. In a large saucepan, mix together white sugar, ¼ cup flour, and salt. Stir in cranberries and maple syrup. Cook over high heat, stirring constantly. When mixture comes to a boil, reduce heat, cover, and simmer 5 minutes, stirring occasionally.

3. Stir apples into simmering mixture, and continue to cook for 5 minutes, or until apples are tender. Remove from heat, and stir in walnuts. Pour apple mixture into pie shell; set aside.

4. In a medium bowl, combine bread crumbs, ¾ cup flour, brown sugar, and melted butter. Mix well, and sprinkle over apple filling.

5. Bake 30 minutes in the preheated oven, or until topping is golden brown. Serve warm.

Yummy Eggnog Pie

Submitted by: **Rodney**

Makes: 1 - 9 inch pie

Preparation: 30 minutes

Cooking: 15 minutes

Ready In: 4 hours 45 minutes

"A yummy delight which has become a holiday tradition in our family as it will in yours! It is surprisingly easy to prepare! Rum may be omitted or substituted with 1 teaspoon rum extract."

INGREDIENTS

1 (4.6 ounce) package cook and serve vanilla pudding mix

1/4 teaspoon ground nutmeg

1 1/2 cups eggnog

2 teaspoons rum

2 cups heavy cream

1 (9 inch) pie shell, baked

1 pinch ground nutmeg

DIRECTIONS

1. In a medium saucepan, combine pudding mix, 1/4 teaspoon nutmeg, and egg nog; mix well. Cook over medium heat, stirring constantly, until thick and bubbly. Remove from heat, and stir in rum. Transfer mixture to a large bowl, cover, and refrigerate until thoroughly chilled.

2. In a medium bowl, whip the cream to soft peaks. Remove the cold pudding from the refrigerator, and beat until smooth; fold in whipped cream. Spoon into baked pie shell. Sprinkle additional nutmeg over the top for garnish. Refrigerate 4 hours, or until set.

Chocolate Rum Mousse Pie

Submitted by: **Karin Christian**

Makes: 1 - 9 inch pie

Preparation: 20 minutes

Ready In: 2 hours 20 minutes

"An easy, elegant, and deliciously creamy no-bake pie. It takes just minutes to assemble, but is an impressive addition to your holiday dessert lineup. Don't like rum? Just omit it, and you will still have a rich and delicious chocolate mousse pie! Garnish with chocolate shavings, and some plastic holly leaves for a pretty presentation."

INGREDIENTS

1 (.25 ounce) package unflavored gelatin

1 tablespoon cold water

2 tablespoons boiling water

1/2 cup white sugar

1/4 cup cocoa

1 (3.9 ounce) package instant chocolate pudding mix

2 cups heavy cream, chilled

1 teaspoon vanilla extract

1 teaspoon rum flavored extract

1 (9 inch) chocolate cookie crumb crust

1 cup heavy cream, chilled

2 tablespoons confectioners' sugar

2 teaspoons rum flavored extract

DIRECTIONS

1. In a small bowl, sprinkle gelatin onto cold water; let stand 1 minute to soften. Stir in boiling water until gelatin is completely dissolved. It must be in liquid form when you add it to the pie filling. If it stiffens up, microwave for about 10 to 15 seconds, and then stir until lump free.

2. In a large bowl, combine sugar, cocoa, and pudding mix. Stir in 2 cups cream, vanilla, and 1 teaspoon rum extract. Beat for 30 seconds with an electric mixer on low, then beat on high until stiff peaks form. Gradually mix in gelatin mixture until blended. Pour filling into pie crust.

3. In a small, chilled bowl, beat 1 cup cream with confectioners' sugar and 2 teaspoons rum extract until stiff peaks form. Spread over chocolate filling. Chill at least 2 hours before slicing and serving.

Chocolate Peanut Butter Pie

Submitted by: **Anna**

Makes: 2 - 8 inch pies

Preparation: 20 minutes

Ready In: 2 hours 20 minutes

"Graham Cracker Crust with a creamy peanut butter layer, a chocolate pudding layer, and a whipped topping layer. Very good but also very rich!"

INGREDIENTS

1 cup peanut butter

3/4 cup butter

3 cups confectioners' sugar

2 (8 inch) prepared graham cracker crusts

2 cups milk

1 (3.9 ounce) package instant chocolate pudding mix

1 (8 ounce) container frozen whipped topping, thawed

DIRECTIONS

1. In a medium, microwave-safe bowl, combine butter and peanut butter. Heat in the microwave until soft; mix well. Gradually stir in confectioners' sugar until the mixture resembles a soft dough. Spread mixture into 2 pie crusts.

2. In a small bowl, mix the milk with the instant pudding. Pour over the peanut butter mixture in each crust. Chill until firm.

3. Top pies with whipped topping when ready to serve.

Apple Dumpling Cake

Submitted by: **Amy S.**

Makes: 1 - 9x13 inch cake

Preparation: 20 minutes

Cooking: 45 minutes

Ready In: 1 hour 5 minutes

"This recipe tastes like apple dumplings without all the work."

INGREDIENTS

3 pounds apples - peeled, cored and sliced

2 cups all-purpose flour

1½ cups white sugar

2 teaspoons baking powder

1 teaspoon salt

2 eggs, beaten

1 cup vegetable oil

1 teaspoon ground cinnamon

DIRECTIONS

1. Preheat oven to 350°F (175°C). Lightly grease a 9x13 inch baking dish.

2. Place sliced apples in baking dish. In a medium bowl, mix together the flour, sugar, baking powder, and salt. Stir in eggs and oil; pack on top of apples. Sprinkle with cinnamon.

3. Bake in preheated oven for 40 to 45 minutes, or until topping is puffed and golden brown.

Apple Cranberry Crisp

Submitted by: **Angie Hammond**

Makes: 1 - 8x8 inch dish

Preparation: 30 minutes

Cooking: 30 minutes

Ready In: 1 hour

"A great combination of apples and cranberries with a crispy topping. A favorite at Thanksgiving instead of plain cranberries."

INGREDIENTS

1 1/2 cups quick cooking oats

1/2 cup brown sugar

1/3 cup all-purpose flour

1 teaspoon ground cinnamon

1/3 cup butter flavored shortening, melted

1 tablespoon water

1 (16 ounce) can whole berry cranberry sauce

2 tablespoons cornstarch

5 Granny Smith apples - peeled, cored and thinly sliced

DIRECTIONS

1. Preheat oven to 375 °F (190°C).

2. In a medium bowl, mix together the oats, brown sugar, flour, and cinnamon. Stir in the melted shortening and water to form a crumbly mixture.

3. In a large saucepan, mix together the cranberry sauce and cornstarch. Bring to a boil, and then remove from heat. Stir in the apples. Spread into an 8x8 inch glass baking dish. Crumble the oat mixture over the apples.

4. Bake in the preheated oven for 30 to 35 minutes, or until the apples are tender. Serve warm.

Pumpkin Crunch Cake

Submitted by: **Nora LaCroix**

Makes: 1 - 9x13 inch cake

Preparation: 15 minutes

Cooking: 1 hour

Ready In: 1 hour 15 minutes

"A great tasting cake, and really easy to make!"

INGREDIENTS

1 (15 ounce) can pumpkin puree

1 (12 fluid ounce) can evaporated milk

4 eggs

1 1/2 cups white sugar

2 teaspoons pumpkin pie spice

1 teaspoon salt

1 (18.25 ounce) package yellow cake mix

1 cup chopped pecans

1 cup margarine, melted

1 (8 ounce) container frozen whipped topping, thawed

DIRECTIONS

1. Preheat oven to 350°F (175°C). Lightly grease one 9x13 inch baking pan.

2. In a large bowl, combine pumpkin, evaporated milk, eggs, sugar, pumpkin pie spice, and salt. Mix well, and spread into the prepared pan.

3. Sprinkle cake mix over the top of the pumpkin mixture, and pat down. Sprinkle chopped pecans evenly over the cake mix, then drizzle with melted margarine.

4. Bake for 60 to 80 minutes, or until done. Top with whipped topping when ready to serve.

Vanilla and Chocolate Delight

Submitted by: **Brenda Moore**

Makes: 1 - 9x13 inch pan

Preparation: 20 minutes

Cooking: 25 minutes

Ready In: 45 minutes

"This makes a delicious dessert that is layers of pecans, cream cheese, and vanilla and chocolate pudding."

INGREDIENTS

1 cup finely chopped pecans

1 cup all-purpose flour

1/2 cup butter, melted

1 (8 ounce) package cream cheese, softened

1 cup confectioners' sugar

1 (16 ounce) container frozen whipped topping, thawed, divided

3 cups milk

1 (3 ounce) package instant chocolate pudding mix

1 (3.5 ounce) package instant vanilla pudding mix

2 (1.45 ounce) bars milk chocolate with crispy rice, crumbled

DIRECTIONS

1. Preheat oven to 400°F (200°C). In a medium mixing bowl, combine pecans, flour, and butter. Press into a 9x13 inch pan. Bake for 25 minutes. Allow to cool.

2. In a large bowl, beat together cream cheese and confectioners' sugar until smooth. Fold in half of the whipped topping. Spread on top of cooled crust.

3. In a large bowl, combine milk, chocolate pudding mix, and vanilla pudding mix. Beat until thick. Pour over cream cheese layer. Top with remaining whipped topping, and sprinkle with crushed chocolate bars.

Pink Stuff

Submitted by: **Shannon**

Makes: 10 servings

Preparation: 10 minutes

Ready In: 3 hours 10 minutes

"This has been used as a Thanksgiving favorite in my family for years. We haven't figured out yet if it's a fruit salad or a dessert! It is rich and good."

INGREDIENTS

1 (21 ounce) can cherry pie filling

1 (14 ounce) can sweetened condensed milk

1 (20 ounce) can crushed pineapple, drained

1 cup chopped pecans

1 (12 ounce) container frozen whipped topping, thawed

DIRECTIONS

1. In a large bowl, mix together pie filling, sweetened condensed milk, crushed pineapple, and pecans. Fold in the whipped topping. Refrigerate until chilled.

Bread Pudding

Submitted by: **Nancy**

Makes: 1 - 2 quart baking dish

Preparation: 20 minutes

Cooking: 30 minutes

Ready In: 50 minutes

"A no frills bread pudding. This is a recipe my mom always made and we all really enjoyed it."

INGREDIENTS

10 slices white bread, cut into cubes

1/4 cup margarine, melted

1/2 cup raisins

1 teaspoon ground cinnamon

6 eggs

3/4 cup white sugar

2 teaspoons vanilla extract

1/2 teaspoon salt

3 cups hot milk

1 pinch ground nutmeg

DIRECTIONS

1. Heat oven to 375°F(190°C)

2. In a large bowl, combine bread cubes, melted margarine, raisins, and cinnamon; mix well, and transfer to a 2 quart baking dish.

3. Use the same bowl to beat the eggs. Stir in sugar, vanilla, and salt until sugar is dissolved. Slowly whisk in the hot milk. Pour egg mixture over bread cubes, sprinkle with nutmeg, and set aside to soak for 5 minutes.

4. Bake in preheated oven for 25 to 30 minutes, or until a knife inserted into the center comes out clean.

Bread Pudding II

Submitted by: **Karen**

Makes: 1 - 8x8 inch dish

Preparation: 20 minutes

Cooking: 50 minutes

Ready In: 1 hour 10 minutes

"This recipe is enjoyed by everyone I have ever served it to. There are never any leftovers because it is so creamy and rich."

INGREDIENTS

2 tablespoons butter, softened

2 1/2 cups cubed day old French bread

4 eggs, beaten

1/2 cup white sugar

1 teaspoon vanilla extract

2 cups milk, scalded

1 pinch ground nutmeg

1 tablespoon dark brown sugar

1 cup pecans, chopped (optional)

DIRECTIONS

1. Preheat oven to 300°F (150°C). Generously butter an 8x8 inch baking dish. Prepare a water bath for the baking dish by placing a larger dish in the oven, and partially filling it with hot water.

2. Place bread cubes in the baking dish. In a medium bowl, beat together eggs, sugar, and vanilla. Slowly whisk in the scalded milk. Pour over the bread. Sprinkle with nutmeg, brown sugar, and pecans.

3. Place the baking dish in the water bath. Bake for 50 to 60 minutes, or until a knife inserted in the middle comes out clean. Serve either hot or chilled.

Chocolate Bar Fondue

Submitted by: **Sara**

Makes: 6 cups

Preparation: 5 minutes

Cooking: 15 minutes

Ready In: 20 minutes

"A rich chocolate fondue with a little coffee kick. Serve with fruit, or pieces of leftover cake on skewers."

INGREDIENTS

32 ounces milk chocolate, grated

1 1/4 cups heavy cream

1 tablespoon instant coffee powder

1 teaspoon vanilla extract

1 teaspoon white sugar

1/3 cup hot water

DIRECTIONS

1. In a saucepan over medium heat, melt the chocolate with the heavy cream. Mix in the instant coffee, vanilla extract, sugar, and hot water. Continue to heat, stirring frequently, until the mixture is smooth.

Lime Gelatin Salad

Submitted by: **Karen Kumar**

Makes: 10 servings

Preparation: 20 minutes

Cooking: 5 minutes

Ready In: 4 hours 25 minutes

"This is a great recipe my mom got from my aunt. She has made it every year for Thanksgiving. It is a family tradition for us. It can be made a day or two ahead of time, if you like. It looks just beautiful in a cut crystal bowl. Thanksgiving is not the same without it for us! We just 'gobble' it up! Chopped walnuts can be substituted for chopped pecans."

INGREDIENTS

1 cup boiling water

1 (6 ounce) package lime flavored gelatin mix

1 (20 ounce) can crushed pineapple, drained with juice reserved

1 (8 ounce) package cream cheese, softened

2 cups heavy cream

1 cup chopped pecans

DIRECTIONS

1. In a large bowl, pour 1 cup boiling water over the gelatin mix. Stir until dissolved, then stir in ½ cup pineapple juice. Refrigerate until thickened but not set, about 1 hour.

2. Meanwhile, place crushed pineapple and remaining juice in a small saucepan. Bring to a boil, reduce heat, and simmer for about 5 minutes. Remove from heat, and cool to room temperature.

3. In a large bowl, blend softened cream cheese and lime gelatin until smooth. Mix in the cooled pineapple. In a medium bowl, whip cream until soft peaks form. Fold into gelatin mixture. Fold in chopped nuts. Pour into a pretty crystal bowl, and refrigerate for at least 4 hours, or until set.

Cranberry Apple Gelatin Mold

Submitted by: **Robyn Schwartz**

Makes: 12 servings

Preparation: 10 minutes

Cooking: 10 minutes

Ready In: 8 hours 20 minutes

"Try this delicious cranberry recipe with a pork roast, too!"

INGREDIENTS

1 (16 ounce) can whole cranberry sauce

1 cup water

2 (3 ounce) packages raspberry flavored gelatin mix

1/4 teaspoon salt

2 apples, cored and diced with peel

2 oranges, peeled, sectioned, and chopped

1/2 cup chopped walnuts

1 cup lemon yogurt

DIRECTIONS

1. In a saucepan over medium heat, combine cranberry sauce and water. Heat until sauce melts. Stir in gelatin until it dissolves. Remove from heat. Mix in apples, oranges, walnuts, and yogurt.

2. Pour mixture into a fancy gelatin mold or a nice bowl, and refrigerate overnight. To serve, dip briefly in hot water, and invert onto a serving dish.

Bing Cherry Gelatin Mold

Submitted by: **Andee**

Makes: 8 servings

Preparation: 5 minutes

Cooking: 10 minutes

Ready In: 24 hours 15 minutes

"Cherry gelatin mold with Bing cherries, pineapple, and pecans. This has been my family's favorite for Thanksgiving for many, many years."

INGREDIENTS

1 (16.5 ounce) can pitted Bing cherries, drained, juice reserved

1 (12 fluid ounce) can cola-flavored carbonated beverage

1 (6 ounce) package black cherry flavored gelatin mix

1 (15.25 ounce) can crushed pineapple, drained

1 cup chopped pecans

DIRECTIONS

1. In a saucepan, combine the reserved cherry juice with the cola. Bring to a boil, and stir in the gelatin until dissolved. Remove from the heat, and mix in the drained cherries, drained pineapple, and chopped pecans. Pour mixture into a mold sprayed with non-stick cooking spray, and refrigerate for at least 24 hours before serving.

candy and cookies

Delightful candies and cookies made by loving friends and relatives are the foundation of so many holiday traditions. Experience the fun passed down through the generations with these tried and true sweet sensations. You'll probably find some of your old favorites in this group, as well as a few new ones that are sure to become a cherished part of your recipe box. Grab a friend and try something new *together!*

Microwave Oven Peanut Brittle

Submitted by: **Linda C.**

Makes: 1 pound

Preparation: 10 minutes

Cooking: 20 minutes

Ready In: 30 minutes

"I have used this for years and it is very good; much easier than the traditional method and tastes just as good."

INGREDIENTS

1½ cups dry roasted peanuts

1 cup white sugar

½ cup light corn syrup

1 pinch salt (optional)

1 tablespoon butter

1 teaspoon vanilla extract

1 teaspoon baking soda

DIRECTIONS

1. Grease a baking sheet, and set aside. In a glass bowl, combine peanuts, sugar, corn syrup, and salt. Cook in microwave for 6 to 7 minutes on High (700 W); mixture should be bubbly and peanuts browned. Stir in butter and vanilla; cook 2 to 3 minutes longer.

2. Quickly stir in baking soda, just until mixture is foamy. Pour immediately onto greased baking sheet. Let cool 15 minutes, or until set. Break into pieces, and store in an airtight container.

Almond Crunch

Submitted by: **Heather**

Makes: 2 pounds

Preparation: 15 minutes

Cooking: 30 minutes

Ready In: 2 hours 20 minutes

"I am begged for this recipe whenever I serve it. My advice: Invest in a good candy thermometer and always, always, always use good ingredients. Do not use margarine as a substitute for the butter; the water content is too high."

INGREDIENTS

1 cup blanched slivered almonds

1 cup butter

1¹/₄ cups white sugar

2 tablespoons light corn syrup

2 tablespoons water

2 cups milk chocolate chips

DIRECTIONS

1. Preheat oven to 375°F (190°C). Arrange almonds in a single layer on a baking sheet. Toast in the preheated oven until lightly browned, approximately 5 minutes.

2. Line a jelly roll pan with foil.

3. In a heavy saucepan, combine butter, sugar, corn syrup, and water. Cook over medium heat, stirring constantly, until mixture boils. Boil, without stirring, to hard crack stage, 300°F (150°C). Remove from heat.

4. Working quickly, stir in almonds, and pour mixture into foil lined jelly roll pan; tip pan from side to side to spread candy evenly in pan. Sprinkle chocolate chips over candy brittle. Let stand about 5 minutes, or until shiny and soft. Spread chocolate evenly over candy. Cool to room temperature, then refrigerate for 1 hour. Break into bite-size pieces.

Peppermint Brittle

Submitted by: **Brenda Moore**

Makes: 2¹/₄ pounds

Preparation: 5 minutes

Cooking: 5 minutes

Ready In: 1 hour 10 minutes

"A Christmastime treat! This holiday confection is gobbled up quickly by guests, and it is so easy to make. The cool crunch of peppermint with creamy white chocolate is a divine combination."

INGREDIENTS

2 pounds white chocolate

30 small peppermint candy canes

DIRECTIONS

1. Line a large jellyroll pan with heavy-duty foil.

2. Place white chocolate in a microwave-safe bowl. Heat in microwave on medium setting for 5 to 6 minutes. Stir occasionally, until chocolate is melted and smooth.

3. Place candy canes in a plastic bag, or between two pieces of waxed paper. Using a mallet or rolling pin, break the candy canes into chunks. Stir peppermint into melted white chocolate. Spread evenly in pan, and chill until set, about 1 hour. Break into pieces by slamming pan on counter.

Almond Buttercrunch Candy

Submitted by: **Janis**

Makes: 3 1/2 pounds

Preparation: 10 minutes

Cooking: 20 minutes

Ready In: 2 hours 30 minutes

"This recipe has been in our family for years, and it is our favorite. It is delicious and addicting. Get ready to go on a diet after the holidays!"

INGREDIENTS

2 (11.5 ounce) packages milk chocolate chips, divided

2 cups butter

1 pound brown sugar

1 cup blanched slivered almonds, divided

DIRECTIONS

1. Preheat oven to 200°F (95°C). Grease a 14 x 18 inch cookie sheet.

2. Sprinkle one package of chocolate chips on prepared pan. Place in warm oven until chips melt, about 5 minutes. Remove from oven, and spread melted chocolate over bottom of pan; set aside.

3. In a large heavy saucepan over medium-high heat, combine butter and brown sugar. Stirring constantly, heat to 300 to 310°F (149 to 154°C), or until a small amount of syrup dropped into cold water forms hard, brittle threads. Immediately remove from heat. Stir in ¾ cup slivered almonds and pour onto pan with melted chocolate; spread mixture evenly.

4. Sprinkle remaining package of chocolate chips over the almond layer. The heat from the almond layer will melt the chocolate chips; spread melted chocolate evenly. Sprinkle remaining ¼ cup almonds over chocolate.

5. Cut into squares, or allow to harden in a solid sheet and break it apart like brittle. Cool completely before removing from pan.

Divinity

Submitted by: **Lisa H.**

Makes: 1 1/2 dozen

Preparation: 20 minutes

Cooking: 30 minutes

Ready In: 50 minutes

"This is a soft white candy made with light corn syrup."

INGREDIENTS

2 cups white sugar

1/2 cup light corn syrup

1/2 cup hot water

1/4 teaspoon salt

2 egg whites

1 teaspoon vanilla extract

DIRECTIONS

1. In a heavy, 2 quart saucepan, combine the sugar, corn syrup, hot water, and salt. Cook and stir until the sugar dissolves and the mixture comes to a boil. Then cook to hard ball stage without stirring, 250°F (120°C.) Frequently wipe crystals forming on the sides of the pan, using a pastry brush dipped in water. Remove from heat.

2. Just as the syrup is reaching temperature, begin whipping egg whites: In a large glass or stainless steel mixing bowl, beat egg whites until stiff peaks form. Pour hot syrup in a thin stream over beaten egg whites, beating constantly with the electric mixer at medium speed. Increase speed to high, and continue beating for about 5 minutes. Add vanilla; continue beating until the mixture becomes stiff and begins to lose its gloss. If it is too stiff, add a few drops hot water.

3. Immediately drop by teaspoonfuls onto waxed paper. For a decorative flair, twirl the top with the spoon when dropping. Let stand until set. Store in an airtight container at room temperature.

Hard Rock Candy

Submitted by: **Pam Lowe**

Makes: 3 pounds

Preparation: 15 minutes

Cooking: 45 minutes

Ready In: 2 hours

"Spicy, cinnamon flavored hard candy. Wrap pieces of it in decorative bags for perfect stocking stuffers. You can vary the flavor by substituting lemon, orange, anise, or other oils. These flavored oils can be found in candy making supply stores and drugstores."

INGREDIENTS

1 cup confectioners' sugar

3³/₄ cups white sugar

1¹/₂ cups light corn syrup

1 cup water

2 teaspoons cinnamon oil

1 teaspoon red food coloring

DIRECTIONS

1. Roll the edges of two 16 inch square pieces of heavy duty aluminum foil. Sprinkle the foil very generously with confectioners' sugar.

2. In a large heavy saucepan, combine the white sugar, corn syrup, and water. Heat over medium-high heat, stirring constantly until sugar dissolves. Stop stirring, and boil until a candy thermometer reads 300 to 310°F (149 to 154°C). Remove from heat.

3. Stir in the cinnamon oil and food coloring. Pour onto the prepared foil, and allow to cool and harden. Crack into pieces, and store in an airtight container.

Cream Cheese Mints

Submitted by: **Diane**

Makes: 8 dozen

Preparation: 30 minutes

Ready In: 2 hours 30 minutes

"These seem to be everyone's favorite holiday candy recipe. Could be the melt in your mouth texture, or perhaps the sweet peppermint taste. Could also be the fact that this is the easiest candy recipe around! If stored in airtight container, these can be frozen for a couple months. These can also be made into pretty shapes by rolling in granulated sugar, pressing into candy molds, and dropping them out."

INGREDIENTS

1 (3 ounce) package cream cheese, softened

1 tablespoon butter, softened

3 cups confectioners' sugar

2 drops peppermint oil

any color food coloring paste (optional)

DIRECTIONS

1. In a large bowl, combine cream cheese, butter, and confectioner's sugar. Mix in peppermint oil. Color as desired with food coloring paste, or leave white.

2. Roll mixture into small balls, and place on waxed paper. Flatten with a fork dipped in confectioners' sugar. Let dry for about 2 hours on waxed paper, then freeze or refrigerate.

Chocolate Covered Peppermint Patties

Submitted by: **Wendy MacLeod**

Makes: 4 dozen

Preparation: 45 minutes

Cooking: 5 minutes

Ready In: 8 hours 50 minutes

"These cool peppermint patties are made with mashed potatoes."

INGREDIENTS

1 cup mashed potatoes

1 teaspoon salt

2 tablespoons melted butter

2 teaspoons peppermint extract

8 cups confectioners' sugar

8 (1 ounce) squares semisweet chocolate

2 tablespoons shortening

DIRECTIONS

1. In a large bowl, mix together the potatoes, salt, butter, and peppermint extract. Gradually mix in confectioners' sugar; mix in enough to make a workable dough, between 6 and 8 cups.

2. Knead slightly, and roll into cherry-size balls. Flatten balls to form patties. Arrange on sheets of wax paper, and allow to dry overnight.

3. Place chocolate and shortening in a microwave-safe bowl. Heat in microwave, stirring occasionally, until melted and smooth. Dip patties in melted chocolate, and let cool on wax paper.

Chocolate Orange Truffles

Submitted by: **Terry**

Makes: 2 dozen

Preparation: 40 minutes

Cooking: 20 minutes

Ready In: 5 hours 30 minutes

"Use orange liqueur or orange juice to flavor these dipped truffles. This is a very easy recipe, requiring no candy thermometer and no sensitive tempering of the chocolate."

INGREDIENTS

¼ cup unsalted butter

3 tablespoons heavy cream

4 (1 ounce) squares semisweet chocolate, chopped

2 tablespoons orange liqueur

1 teaspoon grated orange zest

4 (1 ounce) squares semisweet chocolate, chopped

1 tablespoon vegetable oil

DIRECTIONS

1. In a medium saucepan over medium-high heat, combine butter and cream. Bring to a boil, and remove from heat. Stir in 4 ounces chopped chocolate, orange liqueur, and orange zest; continue stirring until smooth. Pour truffle mixture into a shallow bowl or a 9X5 in loaf pan. Chill until firm, about 2 hours.

2. Line a baking sheet with waxed paper. Shape chilled truffle mixture by rounded teaspoons into small balls (a melon baller also works well for this part). Place on prepared baking sheet. Chill until firm, about 30 minutes.

3. In the top of a double boiler over lightly simmering water, melt remaining 4 ounces chocolate with the oil, stirring until smooth. Cool to lukewarm.

4. Drop truffles, one at a time, into melted chocolate mixture. Using 2 forks, lift truffles out of the chocolate, allowing any excess chocolate to drip back into the pan before transferring back onto baking sheet. Chill until set.

Cocoa Rum Balls

Submitted by: **Leslie**

Makes: 4 dozen

Preparation: 30 minutes

Ready In: 48 hours 30 minutes

"This delicious smooth confection is an impressive dessert for the holidays. These are wonderful for parties, and perfect for holiday gifts to your loved ones. A half cup of orange juice plus one teaspoon of freshly grated orange peel can be substituted for the rum in this recipe."

INGREDIENTS

1 (12 ounce) package vanilla wafers, crushed

1 1/2 cups chopped nuts

3/4 cup confectioners' sugar

1/4 cup cocoa

1/2 cup light rum

3 tablespoons light corn syrup

1/8 cup confectioners' sugar

DIRECTIONS

1. In a large bowl, combine vanilla wafer crumbs, chopped nuts, 3/4 cup confectioners' sugar, and cocoa. Mix in rum and corn syrup. Shape dough into 1 inch balls; roll in confectioners' sugar.

2. Store rum balls in an airtight container for 2 to 3 days to develop flavor. Roll them again in confectioners' sugar before serving.

Buckeye Balls II

Submitted by: **Allison O'Brien**

Makes: 5 dozen

Preparation: 45 minutes

Cooking: 10 minutes

Ready In: 1 hour 25 minutes

"These are chocolate-covered balls of peanut butter and confectioners' sugar."

INGREDIENTS

1 1/2 cups creamy peanut butter

1/2 cup butter, softened

1 teaspoon vanilla extract

4 cups sifted confectioners' sugar

6 ounces semi-sweet chocolate chips

2 tablespoons shortening

DIRECTIONS

1. Line a baking sheet with waxed paper; set aside.

2. In a medium bowl, mix peanut butter, butter, vanilla, and confectioners' sugar with hands to form a smooth stiff dough. Shape into balls using 2 teaspoons of dough for each ball. Place on prepared pan, and refrigerate.

3. Melt shortening and chocolate together in a metal bowl over a pan of lightly simmering water. Stir occasionally until smooth, and remove from heat.

4. Remove balls from refrigerator. Insert a wooden toothpick into a ball, and dip into melted chocolate. Return to wax paper, chocolate side down, and remove toothpick. Repeat with remaining balls. Refrigerate for 30 minutes to set.

Aunt Teen's Creamy Chocolate Fudge

Submitted by: **Kelly Phillips**

Makes: 3 pounds

Preparation: 10 minutes

Cooking: 20 minutes

Ready In: 30 minutes

"This was my aunt's recipe for fudge, passed down through the family. It's better than any fudge I've ever had at the Jersey shore, and easy enough to whip up in 15 minutes or so."

INGREDIENTS

1 (7 ounce) jar marshmallow creme

1 1/2 cups white sugar

2/3 cup evaporated milk

1/4 cup butter

1/4 teaspoon salt

2 cups milk chocolate chips

1 cup semisweet chocolate chips

1/2 cup chopped nuts

1 teaspoon vanilla extract

DIRECTIONS

1. Line an 8x8 inch pan with aluminum foil. Set aside.

2. In a large saucepan over medium heat, combine marshmallow cream, sugar, evaporated milk, butter and salt. Bring to a full boil, and cook for 5 minutes, stirring constantly.

3. Remove from heat and pour in semisweet chocolate chips and milk chocolate chips. Stir until chocolate is melted and mixture is smooth. Stir in nuts and vanilla. Pour into prepared pan. Chill in refrigerator for 2 hours, or until firm.

Raspberry Truffle Fudge

Submitted by: **Leeza**

Makes: 2¹/₂ pounds
Preparation: 10 minutes
Cooking: 10 minutes
Ready In: 1 hour 20 minutes

"A unforgettable double-layer confection that's absolutely perfect for your true love!"

INGREDIENTS

3 cups semi-sweet chocolate chips

1 (14 ounce) can sweetened condensed milk

1¹/₂ teaspoons vanilla extract

salt to taste

¹/₄ cup heavy cream

¹/₄ cup raspberry flavored liqueur

2 cups semi-sweet chocolate chips

DIRECTIONS

1. Spray a 9x9 inch pan with non-stick cooking spray, and line with wax paper.

2. In a microwave-safe bowl, combine 3 cups chocolate chips and sweetened condensed milk. Heat in microwave until chocolate melts, stirring occasionally. Be careful not to let it scorch. Stir in the vanilla and salt. Spread into pan, and cool to room temperature.

3. In a microwave-safe bowl, combine cream, liqueur, and 2 cups chocolate chips. Heat in microwave until the chocolate melts; stir until smooth. Cool to lukewarm, then pour over the fudge layer. Refrigerate until both layers are completely set, about 1 hour. Cut into 1 inch pieces.

Mint Chocolate Fudge

Submitted by: **Susan**

Makes: 1³/₄ pounds

Preparation: 10 minutes

Cooking: 15 minutes

Ready In: 45 minutes

"If you like chocolate and mint together, and want something to satisfy your sweet tooth, this fudge will definitely do it! White confectioners' coating can be found in candy supply shops, or it is sometimes called Almond Bark."

INGREDIENTS

2 cups semisweet chocolate chips

1 (14 ounce) can sweetened condensed milk, divided

2 teaspoons vanilla extract

1 cup white confectioners' coating

1 tablespoon peppermint extract

1 drop green food coloring (optional)

DIRECTIONS

1. Line an 8 or 9 inch square pan with waxed paper.

2. In heavy saucepan over low heat, melt chocolate chips with 1 cup sweetened condensed milk and vanilla. Spread half of the mixture into prepared pan; chill 10 minutes, or until firm. Reserve remaining chocolate mixture at room temperature.

3. In another heavy saucepan over low heat, melt white confectioners' coating with remaining sweetened condensed milk (mixture will be thick.) Stir in peppermint extract and food coloring. Spread this mixture on chilled chocolate layer; chill 10 minutes, or until firm.

4. Spread reserved chocolate mixture over the mint layer; chill 2 hours, or until firm.

White Chocolate Fudge

Submitted by: **Vicki**

Makes: 2 1/2 pounds
Preparation: 15 minutes
Cooking: 10 minutes
Ready In: 1 hour 25 minutes

"This is the white chocolate lovers' equivalent to heaven. Creamy sweet fudge with pecans. Serve it alongside traditional chocolate fudge for a beautiful presentation."

INGREDIENTS

1 (8 ounce) package cream cheese

4 cups confectioners' sugar

1 1/2 teaspoons vanilla extract

12 ounces white chocolate, chopped

3/4 cup chopped pecans

DIRECTIONS

1. Grease an 8x8 inch baking dish. Set aside.

2. In a medium bowl, beat cream cheese, sugar, and vanilla until smooth.

3. In the top of a double boiler over lightly simmering water, heat white chocolate, stirring until melted and smooth.

4. Fold melted white chocolate and pecans into cream cheese mixture. Spread into prepared baking dish. Chill for 1 hour, then cut into 1 inch squares.

World's Best Peanut Butter Fudge

Submitted by: **Debby**

Makes: 3³/₄ pounds

Preparation: 5 minutes

Cooking: 20 minutes

Ready In: 1 hour 25 minutes

"A friend shared this recipe with me, and it is by far the best fudge recipe I've ever tried. This fudge is too good to only make at Christmas!"

INGREDIENTS

4 cups white sugar

1 cup milk

¹/₂ cup butter

1 (7 ounce) jar marshmallow creme

12 ounces peanut butter

²/₃ cup all-purpose flour

DIRECTIONS

1. Grease a 9x13 inch baking dish, set aside.

2. In a saucepan, combine sugar, milk, and butter. Bring to a boil, and cook 5 minutes. Remove from the heat. Stir in the marshmallow creme and peanut butter. Gradually stir in the flour. Spread into the prepared pan, and let cool.

Snow Flakes

Submitted by: **Jessy Davis**

Makes: 6 dozen

Preparation: 20 minutes

Cooking: 10 minutes

Ready In: 1 hour

"This recipe is for use with a cookie press. Wonderfully soft and more flavorful than the average spritz cookie."

INGREDIENTS

1 cup butter flavored shortening

1 (3 ounce) package cream cheese, softened

1 cup white sugar

1 egg yolk

1 teaspoon vanilla extract

1 teaspoon orange zest

2¹/₂ cups all-purpose flour

¹/₂ teaspoon salt

¹/₄ teaspoon ground cinnamon

DIRECTIONS

1. Preheat oven to 350°F (175°C).

2. In a medium bowl, cream together shortening, cream cheese, and sugar. Beat in egg yolk, vanilla, and orange zest. Continue beating until light and fluffy. Gradually stir in flour, salt, and cinnamon. Fill the cookie press, and form cookies on ungreased cookie sheet.

3. Bake in preheated oven for 10 to 12 minutes. Remove from cookie sheet, and cool on wire racks.

Whipped Shortbread Cookies

Submitted by: **William Anatooskin**

Makes: 3 dozen

Preparation: 15 minutes

Cooking: 20 minutes

Ready In: 35 minutes

"A festive melt in your mouth cookie, and very easy to make."

INGREDIENTS

1 cup butter, softened

1 1/2 cups all-purpose flour

1/2 cup confectioners' sugar

1/4 cup red maraschino cherries, quartered

1/4 cup green maraschino cherries, quartered

DIRECTIONS

1. Preheat oven to 350°F (175°C).

2. In a large bowl, combine butter, flour, and confectioners' sugar. With an electric mixer, beat for 10 minutes, until light and fluffy. Spoon onto cookie sheets, spacing cookies 2 inches apart. Place a piece of maraschino cherry onto the middle of each cookie, alternating between red and green.

3. Bake for 15 to 17 minutes in the preheated oven, or until the bottoms of the cookies are lightly browned. Remove from oven, and let cool on cookie sheet for 5 minutes, then transfer cookies on to wire rack to cool. Store in an airtight container, separating each layer with waxed paper.

Delilah's Frosted Cut-Out Sugar Cookies

Submitted by: **Delilah Lopez**

Makes: 3 dozen

Preparation: 10 minutes

Cooking: 8 minutes

Ready In: 18 minutes

"My Family just loves this sugar cookie recipe. The hardened frosting adds a special touch!"

INGREDIENTS

3/4 cup butter flavored shortening

1 cup white sugar

2 eggs

1 tablespoon milk

1 teaspoon vanilla extract

2 1/2 cups all-purpose flour

1 teaspoon baking powder

1 teaspoon salt

1 tablespoon butter

1 teaspoon vanilla extract

2 1/2 cups confectioners' sugar

3 tablespoons milk

2 drops any color food coloring

DIRECTIONS

1. In a large bowl, cream together the shortening and white sugar until smooth. Beat in the eggs one at a time, then stir in the milk and 1 teaspoon vanilla. Combine the flour, baking powder, and salt; stir into the creamed mixture. Cover dough, and chill for at least one hour.

2. Preheat the oven to 400°F (200°C). Lightly grease cookie sheets, or line with parchment paper. On a lightly floured surface, roll out the dough to ¼ inch in thickness. Cut into desired shapes with cookie cutters. Place cookies 1½ inches apart onto cookie sheets.

3. Bake for 6 to 8 minutes in the preheated oven. Remove cookies from baking sheets to cool on wire racks. Cool completely before frosting.

4. In a small bowl, beat the butter, 1 teaspoon vanilla and confectioners' sugar until smooth. Mix in the milk one tablespoon at a time until a good spreading consistency is reached. Stir in food coloring to desired shade. Decorate cooled cookies, and set on waxed paper to harden.

Classic Gingerbread Cutouts

Submitted by: **Brandi Clark**

Makes: 3 dozen

Preparation: 30 minutes

Cooking: 12 minutes

Ready In: 1 hour

"These cookies are so versatile! They are delicious, naturally low-fat, and even make terrific Christmas ornaments that keep for years. Royal Icing is best for decoration. CAUTION: These cookies have a way of disappearing!"

INGREDIENTS

1/2 cup butter, softened

1/2 cup brown sugar

2/3 cup molasses

2 eggs

4 cups all-purpose flour, divided

1/2 teaspoon baking soda

1/2 teaspoon salt

1/2 teaspoon ground allspice

1/2 teaspoon ground cloves

1/2 teaspoon ground cinnamon

1/2 teaspoon ground ginger

1 pound confectioners' sugar

1/2 teaspoon cream of tartar

3 egg whites

DIRECTIONS

1. Preheat oven to 350°F (175°C).

2. In a large bowl, cream together the butter and brown sugar until smooth. Stir in the molasses and eggs. Combine 1½ cups of the flour, baking soda, salt, allspice, cloves, cinnamon, and ginger; beat into the molasses mixture. Gradually stir in the remaining flour by hand to form a stiff dough.

3. Divide dough into 2 pieces. On a lightly floured surface, roll out dough to 1/8 inch thickness. Cut into desired shapes using cookie cutters. Place cookies 1 inch apart onto ungreased cookie sheets.

4. Bake for 8 to 10 minutes in the preheated oven. Allow cookies to cool on baking sheet for 5 minutes before removing to a wire rack to cool completely.

5. In a medium bowl, sift together confectioners' sugar and cream of tartar. Blend in egg whites. Using an electric mixer on high speed, beat for about 5 minutes, or until mixture is thick and stiff. Keep covered with a moist cloth until ready to frost cookies.

Gingerbread Men

Submitted by: **Kim**

Makes: 2¹/₂ dozen

Preparation: 25 minutes

Cooking: 12 minutes

Ready In: 1 hour 37 minutes

"Doesn't need molasses!!!"

INGREDIENTS

1 (3.5 ounce) package cook and serve butterscotch pudding mix

¹/₂ cup butter

¹/₂ cup packed brown sugar

1 egg

1¹/₂ cups all-purpose flour

¹/₂ teaspoon baking soda

1¹/₂ teaspoons ground ginger

1 teaspoon ground cinnamon

DIRECTIONS

1. In a medium bowl, cream together the dry butterscotch pudding mix, butter, and brown sugar until smooth. Stir in the egg. Combine the flour, baking soda, ginger, and cinnamon; stir into the pudding mixture. Cover, and chill dough until firm, about 1 hour.

2. Preheat the oven to 350°F (175°C). Grease baking sheets. On a floured board, roll dough out to about 1/8 inch thickness, and cut into man shapes using a cookie cutter. Place cookies 2 inches apart on the prepared baking sheets.

3. Bake for 10 to 12 minutes in the preheated oven, until cookies are golden at the edges. Cool on wire racks.

Molasses Cookies

Submitted by: **Brenda Hall**

Makes: 5 dozen

Preparation: 10 minutes

Cooking: 10 minutes

Ready In: 1 hour 20 minutes

"My Mom's recipe and one of my favorites. Spicy and chewy, they store well and can be frozen. Great for gift giving or shipping."

INGREDIENTS

3/4 cup margarine, melted

1 cup white sugar

1 egg

1/4 cup molasses

2 cups all-purpose flour

2 teaspoons baking soda

1/2 teaspoon salt

1 teaspoon ground cinnamon

1/2 teaspoon ground cloves

1/2 teaspoon ground ginger

1/2 cup white sugar

DIRECTIONS

1. In a medium bowl, mix together the melted margarine, 1 cup sugar, and egg until smooth. Stir in the molasses. Combine the flour, baking soda, salt, cinnamon, cloves, and ginger; blend into the molasses mixture. Cover, and chill dough for 1 hour.

2. Preheat oven to 375°F (190°C). Roll dough into walnut sized balls, and roll them in the remaining white sugar. Place cookies 2 inches apart onto ungreased baking sheets.

3. Bake for 8 to 10 minutes in the preheated oven, until tops are cracked. Cool on wire racks.

Christmas Wreaths

Submitted by: **Cathy**

"These Christmas wreaths are made using corn flakes and cinnamon candies. They're fun to make and eat. If the mixture is cooling too quickly, set the pan in a skillet with one inch of very hot water to keep the dough manageable."

INGREDIENTS

1/2 cup butter

30 large marshmallows

1 1/2 teaspoons green food coloring

1 teaspoon vanilla extract

4 cups cornflakes cereal

2 tablespoons cinnamon red hot candies

DIRECTIONS

1. Melt butter in a large saucepan over low heat. Add marshmallows, and cook until melted, stirring constantly. Remove from heat, and stir in the food coloring, vanilla, and cornflakes.

2. Quickly drop heaping tablespoonfuls of the mixture onto waxed paper, and form into a wreath shape with lightly greased fingers. Immediately decorate with red hot candies. Allow to cool to room temperature before removing from waxed paper, and storing in an airtight container.

Jam Thumbprints

Submitted by: **Esther**

Makes: 2 dozen

Preparation: 20 minutes

Cooking: 20 minutes

Ready In: 45 minutes

"Delicious and attractive little cookies, with a thumb indentation filled with preserves. Fill with different colored preserves for an interesting presentation."

INGREDIENTS

2/3 cup butter

1/3 cup white sugar

2 egg yolks

1 teaspoon vanilla extract

1/2 teaspoon salt

1 1/2 cups all-purpose flour

2 egg whites, lightly beaten

3/4 cup finely chopped walnuts

1/3 cup strawberry preserves

DIRECTIONS

1. Preheat oven to 350°F (175°C). Lightly grease cookie sheets, or line with parchment paper.

2. In a large bowl, cream together butter and sugar until light and fluffy. Beat in egg yolks, vanilla, and salt. Gradually mix in flour.

3. Shape dough into ¾ inch balls. Dip in lightly beaten egg whites, then roll in finely chopped walnuts. Place 1 inch apart on prepared cookie sheets. Press down center of each with thumb.

4. Bake for 15 to 17 minutes, or until golden brown. Cool on baking sheet for 5 minutes, then remove to a wire rack to cool completely. Just before serving, fill centers of cookies with strawberry preserves.

Sugared Black Raspberry Tea Cookies

Submitted by: **Jennifer**

Makes: 3 dozen

Preparation: 30 minutes

Cooking: 15 minutes

Ready In: 45 minutes

"Petite, crunchy, black raspberry filled thumbprints, dipped in granulated sugar, and studded with miniature chocolate chips. These cookies freeze well."

INGREDIENTS

1/2 cup butter

1/4 cup packed brown sugar

1/3 cup white sugar

1 teaspoon vanilla extract

3 tablespoons milk

1 1/3 cups all-purpose flour

1/4 cup corn starch

1/4 cup miniature semisweet chocolate chips

3 tablespoons white sugar

1 (10 ounce) jar black raspberry jam

DIRECTIONS

1. Preheat oven to 375°F (190°C). Line baking sheets with parchment paper.

2. In a large bowl, cream butter with brown sugar and 1/3 cup white sugar. Blend in the vanilla and milk. Mix in the flour and corn starch. Stir in the mini chocolate chips.

3. Form the dough into 1 inch balls, and roll in the remaining white sugar. Place on the prepared cookie sheet, about 1½ inches apart. Use your finger or thumb to press straight down into the center of each ball, making a well for the jam. Neatly fill each cookie with a small amount of jam.

4. Bake in preheated oven for 13 to 15 minutes, or until cookies are just beginning to turn golden around the edges. Let cookies cool before eating.

Pecan Tassies

Submitted by: **Carla**

Makes: 5 dozen
Preparation: 25 minutes
Cooking: 15 minutes
Ready In: 40 minutes

"These little tarts are a great hit - and look beautiful on a holiday tray!"

INGREDIENTS

2 cups margarine

4 (3 ounce) packages cream cheese

4 cups all-purpose flour

3 eggs

2 1/2 cups packed brown sugar

3 tablespoons melted butter

1/2 teaspoon vanilla extract

1 pinch salt

1 1/2 cups chopped pecans

DIRECTIONS

1. Preheat the oven to 350°F (175°C).

2. In a medium bowl, mix together the margarine and cream cheese until well blended. Beat in flour, 1 cup at a time, until the mixture forms a smooth dough. Roll into small balls, and press into the bottoms and sides of tart pans or mini muffin pans.

3. In another bowl, mix together the eggs, brown sugar, butter, vanilla, and salt. Stir in the pecans. Use a spoon to fill each of the crusts ⅔ full with the filling mixture.

4. Bake for 15 to 18 minutes in the preheated oven, until shell is light brown, and the filling has puffed up. Cool, and carefully remove from pans.

Pecan Pie Bars

Submitted by: **Marietta Strothmann**

Makes: 3 dozen

Preparation: 20 minutes

Cooking: 45 minutes

Ready In: 1 hour 5 minutes

"These pecan pie bars are great for the children and adults in any family."

INGREDIENTS

3 cups all-purpose flour

1/2 cup white sugar

1/2 teaspoon salt

1 cup margarine

4 eggs

1½ cups light corn syrup

1½ cups white sugar

3 tablespoons margarine, melted

1½ teaspoons vanilla extract

2½ cups chopped pecans

DIRECTIONS

1. Preheat oven to 350°F (175°C). Lightly grease a 10x15 inch jellyroll pan.

2. In a large bowl, stir together the flour, ½ cup sugar, and salt. Cut in 1 cup of margarine until mixture resembles coarse crumbs. Sprinkle the mixture evenly over the prepared pan, and press in firmly.

3. Bake for 20 minutes in the preheated oven.

4. While the crust is baking, prepare the filling. In a large bowl mix together the eggs, corn syrup, 1½ cups sugar, 3 tablespoons margarine, and vanilla until smooth. Stir in the chopped pecans. Spread the filling evenly over the crust as soon as it comes out of the oven.

5. Bake for 25 minutes in the preheated oven, or until set. Allow to cool completely on a wire rack before slicing into bars.

Colonial Pumpkin Bars

Submitted by: **Christine Johnson**

Makes: 3 dozen

Preparation: 15 minutes

Cooking: 35 minutes

Ready In: 1 hour 5 minutes

"Vanilla frosted pumpkin bars with walnuts are the best! These can also be frozen with or without the frosting, for later use."

INGREDIENTS

3/4 cup butter

2 cups white sugar

4 eggs, beaten

1 (15 ounce) can pumpkin puree

2 cups all-purpose flour

2 teaspoons baking powder

1/2 teaspoon baking soda

1/2 teaspoon salt

1 teaspoon ground cinnamon

1/4 teaspoon ground nutmeg

1 cup chopped walnuts

1 (3 ounce) package cream cheese, softened

1/3 cup butter, softened

1 teaspoon vanilla extract

3 cups sifted confectioners' sugar

DIRECTIONS

1. Preheat oven to 350°F (175°C). Butter and flour a 10x15 inch jellyroll pan.

2. In a large bowl, cream together ¾ cup butter and white sugar until light and fluffy. Beat in the eggs one at a time, then stir in the pumpkin. Combine the flour, baking powder, baking soda, salt, cinnamon, and nutmeg; stir into the pumpkin mixture. Mix in walnuts. Spread evenly into the prepared pan.

3. Bake for 30 to 35 minutes in the preheated oven, or until toothpick inserted near the center comes out clean. Cool completely before frosting.

4. In a medium bowl, mix together the cream cheese, ⅓ cup butter, and vanilla until smooth. Gradually blend in sugar, then beat until smooth. Spread over cooled pumpkin bars. Cut into squares.

Chewy Noels

Submitted by: **Beth**

Makes: 1 ¹/₂ dozen

Preparation: 15 minutes

Cooking: 20 minutes

Ready In: 35 minutes

"These bar cookies make fabulous holiday gifts. Serve them on Christmas Eve with hot buttered rum. If you desire a cake textured cookie, use an 8x8 inch square pan. Pecans can be substituted for walnuts."

INGREDIENTS

2 tablespoons butter

1 cup packed brown sugar

5 tablespoons all-purpose flour

¹/₈ teaspoon baking soda

2 eggs, beaten

1 teaspoon vanilla extract

1 cup chopped walnuts

¹/₄ cup confectioners' sugar for dusting

DIRECTIONS

1. Preheat oven to 350°F (175°C). Melt the butter in a 7x11 inch baking dish, and tilt the pan to coat all of the sides; set aside.

2. In a medium bowl, stir together the brown sugar, flour, and baking soda. Mix in the eggs and vanilla until smooth, then stir in the walnuts. Pour over the melted butter.

3. Bake in the preheated oven for 20 minutes, or until the edges begin to brown. Cool, then cut into squares, and dust with confectioners' sugar.

Cranberry Pistachio Biscotti

Submitted by: **Gerry Meyer**

Makes: 3 dozen

Preparation: 25 minutes

Cooking: 45 minutes

Ready In: 1 hour 20 minutes

"The red and green make a great Christmas cookie. Have used other nuts instead of pistachios with success. If your pistachios are salted, omit the 1/4 teaspoon salt from the recipe."

INGREDIENTS

1/4 cup light olive oil

3/4 cup white sugar

2 teaspoons vanilla extract

1/2 teaspoon almond extract

2 eggs

13/4 cups all-purpose flour

1/4 teaspoon salt

1 teaspoon baking powder

1/2 cup dried cranberries

11/2 cups pistachio nuts

DIRECTIONS

1. Preheat the oven to 300°F (150°C).

2. In a large bowl, mix together oil and sugar until well blended. Mix in the vanilla and almond extracts, then beat in the eggs. Combine flour, salt, and baking powder; gradually stir into egg mixture. Mix in cranberries and nuts by hand.

3. Divide dough in half. Form two logs (12x2 inches) on a cookie sheet that has been lined with parchment paper. Dough may be sticky; wet hands with cool water to handle dough more easily.

4. Bake for 35 minutes in the preheated oven, or until logs are light brown. Remove from oven, and set aside to cool for 10 minutes. Reduce oven heat to 275°F (135°C).

5. Cut logs on diagonal into ¾ inch thick slices. Lay on sides on parchment covered cookie sheet. Bake approximately 8 to 10 minutes, or until dry; cool.

breakfast

November and December are busy months, so you'll be pleased to know that our most popular holiday breakfasts can be prepared the night before. Take a shortcut here and there you'll still be able to feed everyone fabulous coffeecake or a hearty breakfast casserole. If you've got a hankering to spend time making a more elaborate, memorable treat, we've got you covered, too.

Yeast Raised Christmas Waffles

Submitted by: **Holly**

Makes: 4 Belgian-style waffles

Preparation: 25 minutes

Cooking: 10 minutes

Ready In: 1 hour 35 minutes

"Raised yeast waffles are the perfect breakfast treat! You may substitute butter-milk for lukewarm milk, but you must add 1 teaspoon of baking soda to the dry ingredients."

INGREDIENTS

1 (.25 ounce) package active dry yeast

2 cups warm milk (110 degrees F/45 degrees C)

2½ cups sifted all-purpose flour

¼ teaspoon salt

1 tablespoon white sugar

4 egg yolks

1 teaspoon vanilla extract

½ cup melted butter

4 egg whites

DIRECTIONS

1. In a small bowl, dissolve yeast in warm milk. Let stand until creamy, about 10 minutes.

2. In a large bowl, mix the flour, salt, and sugar. Beat the egg yolks into the yeast mixture, and mix into the dry ingredients. Stir in the vanilla extract and melted butter.

3. In a large glass or metal bowl, whip egg whites until stiff peaks form. Carefully fold into the waffle batter. Let stand in a warm place about 45 minutes, or until doubled in size.

4. Preheat a Belgian-style waffle iron, and coat with cooking spray. Place ¾ to 1 cup of batter onto the hot iron; close the lid. Cook until the steaming subsides and the waffle is golden brown.

Overnight Raisin Oatmeal Pancakes

Submitted by: **Cindy Carnes**

Makes: 18 pancakes
Preparation: 20 minutes
Cooking: 10 minutes
Ready In: 12 hours 30 minutes

"We prepare these on Christmas Eve to eat for breakfast on Christmas Day before opening our gifts."

INGREDIENTS

2 cups quick-cooking oats

2 cups buttermilk

1/2 cup all-purpose flour

2 tablespoons white sugar

1 teaspoon baking powder

1 teaspoon baking soda

1/2 teaspoon ground cinnamon

1/2 teaspoon salt

2 eggs, beaten

1/4 cup butter, softened

1/3 cup raisins

DIRECTIONS

1. In a medium bowl, mix together the oats and buttermilk. Cover, and refrigerate overnight.

2. The next morning: In a large bowl, sift together the flour, sugar, baking powder, baking soda, cinnamon, and salt. Make a well in the center, and pour in the oatmeal mixture, eggs, butter, and raisins. Stir until just moistened. Allow batter to sit 20 minutes before cooking. If batter is too thick, add buttermilk 1 tablespoon at a time, until the batter reaches the desired consistency.

3. Heat a lightly greased, large skillet or griddle over medium heat. Pour 1/4 cup batter onto the hot griddle for each cake. Cook pancakes until bubbles appear on top, flip, and cook until lightly browned on bottom.

Creme Brulee French Toast

Submitted by: **Sandi**

Makes: 6 servings

Preparation: 20 minutes

Cooking: 40 minutes

Ready In: 9 hours

"Very rich French toast - can be made ahead of time."

INGREDIENTS

1/2 cup unsalted butter

1 cup packed brown sugar

2 tablespoons corn syrup

6 (1 inch thick) slices French bread

5 eggs

1 1/2 cups half-and-half cream

1 teaspoon vanilla extract

1 teaspoon orange brandy

1/4 teaspoon salt

DIRECTIONS

1. Melt butter in a small saucepan over medium heat. Mix in brown sugar and corn syrup, stirring until sugar is dissolved. Pour into a 9x13 inch baking dish.

2. Remove crusts from bread, and arrange in the baking dish in a single layer. In a small bowl, whisk together eggs, half and half, vanilla extract, orange brandy, and salt. Pour over the bread. Cover, and chill at least 8 hours, or overnight.

3. Preheat oven to 350°F (175°C). Remove the dish from the refrigerator, and bring to room temperature.

4. Bake uncovered 35 to 40 minutes in the preheated oven, until puffed and lightly browned.

Overnight Blueberry French Toast

Submitted by: **Karan Cox**

Makes: 10 servings

Preparation: 15 minutes

Cooking: 1 hour 15 minutes

Ready In: 10 hours

"This is a very unique breakfast dish. Good for any holiday breakfast or brunch, it's filled with the fresh taste of blueberries, and covered with a rich blueberry sauce to make it a one of a kind."

INGREDIENTS

12 slices day-old bread, cut into 1 inch cubes

2 (8 ounce) packages cream cheese, cut into 1 inch cubes

1 cup fresh blueberries

12 eggs, beaten

2 cups milk

1 teaspoon vanilla extract

1/3 cup maple syrup

1 cup white sugar

2 tablespoons cornstarch

1 cup water

1 cup fresh blueberries

1 tablespoon butter

DIRECTIONS

1. Lightly grease a 9x13 inch baking dish. Arrange half the bread cubes in the dish, and top with cream cheese cubes. Sprinkle 1 cup blueberries over the cream cheese, and top with remaining bread cubes.

2. In a large bowl, mix the eggs, milk, vanilla extract, and syrup. Pour over the bread cubes. Cover, and refrigerate overnight.

3. Remove the bread cube mixture from the refrigerator about 30 minutes before baking. Preheat the oven to 350°F (175°C).

4. Cover, and bake 30 minutes. Uncover, and continue baking 25 to 30 minutes, until center is firm and surface is lightly browned.

5. In a medium saucepan, mix the sugar, cornstarch, and water. Bring to a boil. Stirring constantly, cook 3 to 4 minutes. Mix in the remaining 1 cup blueberries. Reduce heat, and simmer 10 minutes, until the blueberries burst. Stir in the butter, and pour over the baked French toast

Christmas Breakfast Sausage Casserole

Submitted by: **M.K. Meredith**

Makes: 8 servings

Preparation: 20 minutes

Cooking: 1 hour 30 minutes

Ready In: 9 hours 50 minutes

"My mom has always made this for us on Christmas morning, and since we only have it once a year it makes it even more good. It is so delicious, and everyone enjoys it! When I double the recipe I use 1 pound regular sausage and 1 pound sage sausage."

INGREDIENTS

1 pound ground pork sausage

1 teaspoon mustard powder

1/2 teaspoon salt

4 eggs, beaten

2 cups milk

6 slices white bread, toasted and cut into cubes

8 ounces mild Cheddar cheese, shredded

DIRECTIONS

1. Crumble sausage into a medium skillet. Cook over medium heat until evenly brown; drain.

2. In a medium bowl, mix together mustard powder, salt, eggs and milk. Add the sausage, bread cubes, and cheese, and stir to coat evenly. Pour into a greased 9x13 inch baking dish. Cover, and chill in the refrigerator for 8 hours, or overnight.

3. Preheat oven to 350°F (175°C).

4. Cover, and bake 45 to 60 minutes. Uncover, and reduce temperature to 325°F (165°C). Bake for an additional 30 minutes, or until set.

Breakfast Casserole II

Submitted by: **Sue Schuler**

Makes: 12 servings

Preparation: 15 minutes

Cooking: 1 hour

Ready In: 1 hour 15 minutes

"A great holiday breakfast casserole that may be made the night before, and baked while opening Christmas presents."

INGREDIENTS

1 (16 ounce) package ground pork breakfast sausage

12 eggs

1 (10.75 ounce) can condensed cream of mushroom soup

1 (10.75 ounce) can milk

1 (4.5 ounce) can sliced mushrooms, drained

1 (32 ounce) package frozen potato rounds

1/2 cup shredded Cheddar cheese

DIRECTIONS

1. Place sausage in a skillet over medium-high heat, and cook until evenly brown. Drain, and set aside.

2. Preheat oven to 350°F (175°C). Lightly grease a 9x13 inch baking dish.

3. In a large bowl, beat together the eggs, condensed cream of mushroom soup, and milk. Stir in the sausage and mushrooms, and pour into the prepared baking dish. Mix in the frozen potato rounds.

4. Bake in preheated oven for 45 to 50 minutes. Sprinkle with cheese, and bake an additional 10 minutes, or until cheese is melted.

Cheddar Quiche

Submitted by: **Jennifer**

Makes: 1 - 9 inch pie

Preparation: 20 minutes

Cooking: 40 minutes

Ready In: 1 hour

"The crust is made with baking mix, so it is heartier than a flaky pastry. Serve warm or at room temperature."

INGREDIENTS

1 cup all-purpose baking mix

¼ teaspoon salt

¼ teaspoon ground black pepper

⅓ cup milk

3 slices bacon, chopped

1 small onion, chopped

2 cups shredded Cheddar cheese

4 eggs

1 teaspoon salt

¼ teaspoon hot pepper sauce

1 (12 fluid ounce) can evaporated milk, heated

DIRECTIONS

1. Preheat oven to 400°F (200°C). Lightly grease a 9 inch pie pan.

2. In a medium bowl, mix together the baking mix, ¼ teaspoon salt, and pepper. Gradually mix in the milk until moistened. Knead a few times on a floured board. Roll dough out to a 12 inch circle, and press into the greased pie pan. Fold edges, and flute.

3. Place bacon and onion in a large, deep skillet over medium-high heat, and cook until bacon is evenly brown. Drain, and crumble bacon. Sprinkle bacon, onion, and Cheddar cheese into the pie pan.

4. In a medium bowl, beat eggs with 1 teaspoon salt and hot pepper sauce, then slowly stir in hot evaporated milk. Pour into the pie shell.

5. Bake 5 minutes in the preheated oven, then reduce heat to 350°F (175°C). Continue baking 25 minutes, or until center is almost set. Do not over bake - the quiche will set as it cools.

Bacon Quiche Tarts

Submitted by: **Donna**

Makes: 10 tarts

Preparation: 15 minutes

Cooking: 25 minutes

Ready In: 40 minutes

"Light and flaky, these tarts are easy to make and easy to reheat. Just wrap loosely in foil and heat at 350 degrees F for 10 to 15 minutes, or until warm."

INGREDIENTS

5 slices bacon

1 (8 ounce) package cream cheese, softened

2 tablespoons milk

2 eggs

1/2 cup shredded Swiss cheese

2 tablespoons chopped green onion

1 (10 ounce) can refrigerated flaky biscuit dough

DIRECTIONS

1. Preheat oven to 375°F (190°C). Lightly grease 10 muffin cups.

2. Place bacon in a large, deep skillet. Cook over medium high heat until crisp and evenly brown. Drain, crumble, and set aside.

3. Place the cream cheese, milk, and eggs in a medium bowl, and beat until smooth with an electric mixer set on Low. Stir in Swiss cheese and green onion, and set aside.

4. Separate dough into 10 biscuits. Press into the bottom and sides of each muffin cup, forming ¼ inch rims. Sprinkle half of the bacon into the bottoms of the dough-lined muffin cups. Spoon about 2 tablespoons of the cream cheese mixture into each cup.

5. Bake 20 to 25 minutes in the preheated oven, until filling is set and rims of the tarts are golden brown. Sprinkle with the remaining bacon, and lightly press into the filling. Remove from pan, and serve warm.

Grandma Johnson's Scones

Submitted by: **Rob**

Makes: 12 scones

Preparation: 15 minutes

Cooking: 15 minutes

Ready In: 30 minutes

"A basic scone recipe that really does the trick. Tried and tested through 3 generations of kids. Simply the best anywhere!"

INGREDIENTS

1 cup sour cream

1 teaspoon baking soda

4 cups all-purpose flour

1 cup white sugar

2 teaspoons baking powder

$^1/_4$ teaspoon cream of tartar

1 teaspoon salt

1 cup butter

1 egg

1 cup raisins (optional)

DIRECTIONS

1. In a small bowl, blend the sour cream and baking soda, and set aside.

2. Preheat oven to 350°F (175°C). Lightly grease a large baking sheet.

3. In a large bowl, mix the flour, sugar, baking powder, cream of tartar, and salt. Cut in the butter. Stir the sour cream mixture and egg into the flour mixture until just moistened. Mix in the raisins.

4. Turn dough out onto a lightly floured surface, and knead briefly. Roll or pat dough into a ¾ inch thick round. Cut into 12 wedges, and place them 2 inches apart on the prepared baking sheet.

5. Bake 12 to 15 minutes in the preheated oven, until golden brown on the bottom.

Scottish Oat Scones

Submitted by: **Carol**

Makes: 16 scones

Preparation: 15 minutes

Cooking: 15 minutes

Ready In: 30 minutes

"These are delicious and won't last long."

INGREDIENTS

1 1/2 cups all-purpose flour

2 cups rolled oats

1/4 cup white sugar

4 teaspoons baking powder

1/2 teaspoon salt

1/2 cup currants

1 egg, beaten

1/2 cup butter, melted

1/3 cup milk

DIRECTIONS

1. Preheat the oven to 425°F (220°C). Lightly grease a baking sheet.

2. In a large bowl, mix the flour, oats, sugar, baking powder, salt, and currants. Make a well in the center. In a small bowl, beat egg until frothy, and stir in melted butter and milk. Pour into the well, and mix to create a soft dough. Pat dough into two 1/2 inch thick circles. Place on the prepared baking sheet. Score 8 wedges into each circle of dough.

3. Bake 15 minutes in the preheated oven, until risen and browned. Split wedges, and serve warm.

Scones

Submitted by: **Donna**

Makes: 8 scones

Preparation: 10 minutes

Cooking: 15 minutes

Ready In: 25 minutes

"This is a very simple recipe for scones. You can customize them by adding dried fruit or nuts. Half and half can also be substituted for milk if you wish."

INGREDIENTS

3 cups all-purpose flour

1/2 cup white sugar

5 teaspoons baking powder

1/2 teaspoon salt

3/4 cup butter

1 egg, beaten

1 cup milk

DIRECTIONS

1. Preheat oven to 400°F (200°C). Lightly grease a baking sheet.

2. In a large bowl, combine flour, sugar, baking powder, and salt. Cut in butter. Mix the egg and milk in a small bowl, and stir into flour mixture until moistened.

3. Turn dough out onto a lightly floured surface, and knead briefly. Roll dough out into a ½ inch thick round. Cut into 8 wedges, and place on the prepared baking sheet.

4. Bake 15 minutes in the preheated oven, or until golden brown.

Cranberry Swirl Coffee Cake

Submitted by: **Laura Owen**

Makes: 1 -9 or 10 inch tube pan

Preparation: 20 minutes

Cooking: 55 minutes

Ready In: 1 hour 15 minutes

"This old family recipe is delicious for breakfast on Thanksgiving day, or to eat while watching the parade! Plain yogurt can be substituted for sour cream."

INGREDIENTS

1/2 cup butter

1 cup white sugar

2 eggs

1 teaspoon almond extract

2 cups all-purpose flour

1 teaspoon baking powder

1 teaspoon baking soda

1/2 teaspoon salt

1 cup sour cream

1 (8 ounce) can whole cranberry sauce

DIRECTIONS

1. Preheat oven to 350°F (175°C). Grease and flour one 9 or 10 inch tube pan.

2. In a large bowl, cream together the butter and sugar until light and fluffy. Beat in the eggs one at a time, then stir in the almond extract. Combine the flour, baking powder, baking soda, and salt; stir into the creamed mixture alternately with the sour cream.

3. Pour 1/3 of the batter into the prepared tube pan. Swirl 1/2 of the cranberry sauce into the batter. Repeat, ending with the batter on top.

4. Bake 55 minutes in the preheated oven, until golden brown.

Overnight Coffee Cake

Submitted by: **Amy Posont**

Makes: 1 -8 inch square cake

Preparation: 15 minutes

Cooking: 45 minutes

Ready In: 9 hours

"When I first got this recipe I thought it would be strange to make this cake, then refrigerate it, and bake the next morning. But it's great. The cake is so moist and delicious. It's wonderful when you have company staying at your house, and it makes a great breakfast with a cup of coffee."

INGREDIENTS

1/3 cup butter, softened	1/4 teaspoon baking soda
1/2 cup white sugar	1/2 teaspoon ground cinnamon
1/4 cup packed brown sugar	1/2 cup buttermilk
1 egg	1/4 cup packed brown sugar
1 cup all-purpose flour	1/4 cup finely chopped walnuts
1/2 teaspoon baking powder	1/4 teaspoon ground cinnamon

DIRECTIONS

1. In a large bowl, cream together the butter, white sugar, and ¼ cup brown sugar. Beat in the egg until well blended. In a medium bowl, combine the flour, baking powder, baking soda, and ½ teaspoon cinnamon. Stir the flour mixture into the creamed mixture alternately with buttermilk. Spread evenly into the prepared baking pan.

2. In a small bowl, mix ¼ cup brown sugar, walnuts, and ¼ teaspoon cinnamon. Sprinkle over the batter. Cover, and refrigerate overnight.

3. Preheat oven to 350°F (175°C). Lightly grease an 8 inch square baking pan.

4. Bake 40 to 45 minutes in the preheated oven, or until a toothpick inserted in the center comes out clean.

Sour Cream Coffee Cake III

Submitted by: Jan Taylor

Makes: 1 - 9x13 inch cake
Preparation: 15 minutes
Cooking: 40 minutes
Ready In: 55 minutes

"This cake is so moist. Enjoy it with a delicious cup of tea or coffee in the morning."

INGREDIENTS

1 cup butter

2 cups white sugar

2 eggs

1 cup sour cream

1/2 teaspoon vanilla extract

2 cups all-purpose flour

1 teaspoon baking powder

1/8 teaspoon salt

1/3 cup all-purpose flour

1/2 cup packed brown sugar

2 tablespoons melted butter

1 teaspoon ground cinnamon

DIRECTIONS

1. Preheat oven to 350°F (175°C). Grease a 9x13 inch baking pan.

2. In a large bowl, cream together 1 cup butter and white sugar until light and fluffy. Beat in the eggs one at a time, then stir in the sour cream and vanilla. Mix in 2 cups flour, baking powder, and salt. Spread ½ of batter in the prepared pan.

3. Prepare the filling: In a medium bowl mix ⅓ cup flour, brown sugar, 2 tablespoons melted butter, and cinnamon. Sprinkle cake batter with ½ the filling. Spread second half of batter over the filling, and top with remaining filling.

4. Bake 35 to 40 minutes in the preheated oven, or until a toothpick inserted near the center comes out clean.

Streusel Apple Coffeecake

Submitted by: **Kris**

Makes: 1 - 9 or 10 inch Bundt cake

Preparation: 30 minutes

Cooking: 1 hour

Ready In: 1 hour 30 minutes

"Wonderfully moist coffee cake with a layer of apples and streusel in the middle and more streusel on top. Very good."

INGREDIENTS

1 1/2 cups packed light brown sugar

3/4 cup all-purpose flour

1/2 cup butter, chilled and diced

2 teaspoons ground cinnamon

1 cup chopped walnuts

3 1/4 cups all-purpose flour

1 1/2 teaspoons baking powder

3/4 teaspoon baking soda

3/4 cup butter, room temperature

1 1/2 cups white sugar

3 eggs

2 teaspoons vanilla extract

16 ounces plain low-fat yogurt

2 Granny Smith apples - peeled, cored and finely diced

DIRECTIONS

1. Preheat oven to 350°F (175°C). Grease and flour a Bundt cake pan.

2. To make streusel: In a medium bowl, mix brown sugar, ¾ cup flour, and cinnamon. Cut in the butter with a fork until crumbly. Stir in walnuts.

3. In a medium bowl, stir together 3¼ cups flour, baking powder, and baking soda. In a large bowl, cream together the butter and sugar until light and fluffy. Beat in the eggs one at a time, mixing well after each. Then stir in the vanilla and yogurt. Gently stir in the flour mixture just until blended.

4. Pour 3 cups of the batter into the Bundt pan, sprinkle with ¼ of the streusel, and layer with apples. Sprinkle with ½ the remaining streusel. Pour in the remaining batter, and top with the remaining ¼ streusel. Lightly pat the top layer of streusel so it sticks to the cake batter.

5. Bake 50 to 60 minutes in the preheated oven, or until a toothpick inserted in the center comes out clean. Cool in the pan on a wire rack 15 minutes. Place cookie sheet over pan and carefully invert both. Remove Bundt pan, and let the cake cool completely.

Christmas Stollen

Submitted by: **Lee Smith**

Makes: 1 loaf

Preparation: 30 minutes

Cooking: 50 minutes

Ready In: 3 hours

"I got this recipe while I was head baker at London's Dorchester Hotel. It's packed with dried fruit and filled with a marzipan surprise."

INGREDIENTS

1 tablespoon active dry yeast

2/3 cup warm milk (110 degrees F/45 degrees C)

1 large egg

1/3 cup white sugar

1/2 tablespoon salt

1/3 cup butter, softened

2 1/2 cups bread flour

1/3 cup currants

1/3 cup golden raisins

1/3 cup red candied cherries, quartered

2/3 cup diced candied citron

6 ounces marzipan

1 tablespoon confectioners' sugar

1 teaspoon ground cinnamon

DIRECTIONS

1. In a small bowl, dissolve yeast in warm milk. Let stand until creamy, about 10 minutes.

2. In a large bowl, combine the yeast mixture with the egg, white sugar, salt, butter, and 2 cups bread flour; beat well. Add the remaining flour, ¼ cup at a time, stirring well after each addition. When the dough has begun to pull together, turn it out onto a lightly floured surface, and knead in the currants, raisins, dried cherries, and citrus peel. Continue kneading until smooth, about 8 minutes.

3. Lightly oil a large bowl, place the dough in the bowl, and turn to coat with oil. Cover with a damp cloth and let rise in a warm place until doubled in volume, about 1 hour.

4. Lightly grease a cookie sheet. Deflate the dough, and turn it out onto a lightly floured surface. Roll the marzipan into a rope, and place it in the center of the dough. Fold the dough over the marzipan; pinch the seams together to seal. Place the loaf, seam side down, on the prepared baking sheet. Cover with a damp cloth, and let rise until doubled in volume, about 40 minutes. Meanwhile, preheat oven to 350°F (175°C).

5. Bake in the preheated oven for 10 minutes. Reduce heat to 300°F (150°C), and bake for 30 to 40 minutes, or until golden brown. Allow loaf to cool on a wire rack. Dust the cooled loaf with confectioners' sugar, and sprinkle with the cinnamon.

Panettone II

Submitted by: **Sandra Chan**

Makes: 1 - 1¹/₂ pound loaf

Preparation: 5 minutes

Cooking: 3 hours

Ready In: 3 hours 5 minutes

"This is an Italian Christmas bread. This recipe is only suitable for the bread machine. I have tried it many times successfully, you will love it."

INGREDIENTS

³/₄ cup warm water

¹/₄ cup butter

2 eggs

1¹/₂ teaspoons vanilla extract

3¹/₄ cups bread flour

2 tablespoons white sugar

2 tablespoons dry milk powder

1¹/₂ teaspoons salt

2 teaspoons bread machine yeast

¹/₂ cup chopped dried mixed fruit

DIRECTIONS

1. Place all of the ingredients except for the mixed fruit into the pan of your bread machine in order directed by manufacturer. Select Sweet or Basic/White bread cycle, and use the Medium or Light crust color. Do not use the delay cycles. Add the fruit 5 to 10 minutes before the last kneading cycle ends, or when the raisin or nut signal starts.

gifts

When the gift-list beckons, you may just want to run for the safety of your kitchen! This year we say: Don't fight that instinct. Give the gift of a satisfied tummy and a warm heart by presenting loved ones with a homemade gift they can tuck into with gusto. We have a special collection of food-gift ideas that will keep on giving throughout the year.

Cranberry Nut Bread

Submitted by: **Karin Christian**

Makes: 1 - 9x5 inch loaf

Preparation: 15 minutes

Cooking: 50 minutes

Ready In: 1 hour 5 minutes

"A moist quick bread with a faint hint of orange flavor, and the tang of bits of cranberries."

INGREDIENTS

2 cups all-purpose flour

3/4 cup white sugar

3/4 teaspoon salt

1 1/2 teaspoons baking powder

1/2 teaspoon baking soda

1 cup chopped cranberries

1/2 cup chopped walnuts

1 egg

2 tablespoons vegetable oil

3/4 cup orange juice

1 tablespoon orange zest

DIRECTIONS

1. Preheat oven to 350°F (175°C). Grease a 9x5 inch loaf pan.

2. Combine the flour, sugar, salt, baking powder, and baking soda. Add the cranberries and walnuts, and stir to coat with flour. Mix together the egg, oil, orange juice, and orange zest. Pour the egg mixture into the flour mixture, and stir until just blended. Spoon the batter into the prepared pan.

3. Bake for 50 minutes in the preheated oven, or until a toothpick inserted near the center comes out clean. Cool in pan for 10 minutes, then remove to a wire rack, and cool completely.

Banana Cranberry Bread

Submitted by: **Linda Vollrath**

Makes: 2 - 9x5 inch loaves

Preparation: 15 minutes

Cooking: 1 hour

Ready In: 1 hour 30 minutes

"I always have leftover cranberry sauce after Thanksgiving, so I created this recipe which is very moist and delicious."

INGREDIENTS

2$1/2$ cups white sugar

1 cup shortening

3 eggs

3 mashed bananas

1 cup cranberry sauce

$1/2$ cup milk

1 teaspoon vanilla extract

4 cups all-purpose flour

$1^{1}/_{2}$ teaspoons baking soda

$1^{1}/_{2}$ teaspoons baking powder

1 teaspoon ground cinnamon

$1/2$ teaspoon ground nutmeg

$1/2$ cup chopped walnuts

DIRECTIONS

1. Preheat oven to 350°F (175°C). Lightly grease two 9x5 inch loaf pans.

2. In a large bowl, cream together the sugar and shortening until light and fluffy. Beat in eggs, and mix in bananas, cranberry sauce, milk, and vanilla. In a separate bowl, mix together flour, baking soda, baking powder, cinnamon, and nutmeg. Gradually blend flour mixture into the banana mixture. Fold in walnuts. Pour into the prepared loaf pans.

3. Bake for 50 to 60 minutes in the preheated oven, or until a toothpick inserted in the center comes out clean. Cool in pan for 10 minutes, then turn out onto a wire rack, and cool completely.

Cranberry Orange Loaf

Submitted by: **Carol**

Makes: 1 - 9x5 inch loaf

Preparation: 15 minutes

Cooking: 1 hour

Ready In: 1 hour 25 minutes

"This is an excellent flavor to choose from. Orange and cranberry flavors will be sure to put you in the holiday spirit. It tastes even better the next day."

INGREDIENTS

2 cups all-purpose flour

1 1/2 teaspoons baking powder

1/2 teaspoon baking soda

1/2 teaspoon salt

1 tablespoon grated orange zest

1 1/2 cups fresh cranberries

1/2 cup pecans, coarsely chopped

1/4 cup margarine, softened

1 cup white sugar

1 egg

3/4 cup orange juice

DIRECTIONS

1. Preheat the oven to 350°F (175°C). Grease and flour a 9x5 inch loaf pan. Whisk together flour, baking powder, baking soda, and salt. Stir in orange zest, cranberries, and pecans. Set aside.

2. In a large bowl, cream together margarine, sugar, and egg until smooth. Stir in orange juice. Beat in flour mixture until just moistened. Pour into prepared pan.

3. Bake for 1 hour in the preheated oven, or until the bread springs back when lightly touched. Let stand 10 minutes, then turn out onto a wire rack to cool. Wrap in plastic when completely cool.

Orange Pumpkin Loaf

Submitted by: **Carol**

Makes: 1 - 9x5 inch loaf

Preparation: 20 minutes

Cooking: 1 hour

Ready In: 1 hour 30 minutes

"You can try this moist loaf with an orange cream spread, butter, or leave plain. For a variation, try substituting dates for the raisins."

INGREDIENTS

1 large orange

1/3 cup butter, softened

1 1/3 cups white sugar

2 eggs

1 cup canned pumpkin

1/3 cup water

2 cups all-purpose flour

1 teaspoon baking soda

1/2 teaspoon baking powder

3/4 teaspoon salt

1/2 teaspoon ground cinnamon

1/2 teaspoon ground cloves

1/2 cup chopped walnuts

1/2 cup chopped raisins

DIRECTIONS

1. Preheat oven to 350°F (175°C). Grease a 9x5 inch loaf pan.

2. Cut orange into wedges, and remove seeds. Place orange, peel and all, in a food processor. Pulse until finely chopped; set aside.

3. In a large bowl, cream butter and sugar until smooth. Beat in the eggs one at a time, then stir in the pumpkin, water, and the ground orange. Mix together flour, baking soda, baking powder, salt, cinnamon, and cloves. Stir into batter just until moistened. Stir in nuts and raisins. Spoon into the prepared loaf pan.

4. Bake for 1 hour in the preheated oven, or until a toothpick inserted near the center comes out clean. Let stand 10 minutes, then remove from pan, and cool on a wire rack.

Super Moist Pumpkin Bread

Submitted by: **Kevin Ryan**

Makes: 2 - 8x4 inch loaves

Preparation: 5 minutes

Cooking: 1 hour 15 minutes

Ready In: 1 hour 30 minutes

"This is an incredible bread. Its moistness comes from the addition of an unusual ingredient: coconut milk! If sweetened coconut is used, reduce white sugar to 1/2 cup."

INGREDIENTS

1 cup chopped walnuts

3¹/2 cups all-purpose flour

2 cups packed dark brown sugar

²/3 cup white sugar

2 teaspoons baking soda

1 teaspoon salt

1 teaspoon ground nutmeg

1¹/2 teaspoons ground cinnamon

2 cups pumpkin puree

1 cup vegetable oil

²/3 cup coconut milk

²/3 cup flaked coconut

DIRECTIONS

1. Preheat oven to 350°F (175°C). Grease and flour two 8x4 inch loaf pans.

2. Spread walnuts in a single layer on an ungreased baking sheet. Toast in the preheated oven for 8 to 10 minutes, or until lightly browned. Set aside to cool.

3. In a large bowl, stir together the flour, brown sugar, white sugar, baking soda, salt, nutmeg, and cinnamon. Add the pumpkin puree, oil, and coconut milk, and mix until all of the flour is absorbed. Fold in the flaked coconut and toasted walnuts. Divide the batter evenly between the prepared pans.

4. Bake for 1 hour and 15 minutes in the preheated oven, or until a toothpick inserted in the center comes out clean. Remove from oven, and cover loaves tightly with foil. Allow to steam for 10 minutes. Remove foil, and turn out onto a cooling rack. Tent loosely with the foil, and allow to cool completely.

Pumpkin Bread IV

Submitted by: **Cheryl Riccioli**

Makes: 3 - 9x5 inch loaves
Preparation: 15 minutes
Cooking: 1 hour
Ready In: 1 hour 15 minutes

"This is an all time, excellent, everytime recipe. It is very simple, and so well loved by many. I make these for family, friends, school functions, work functions, for gifts etc. It has always been raved about - even by kids! I recommend bringing this to your Thanksgiving function; you will be thanked many times for this delicious taste treat. This is a large quantity, but you will end up making this size batch more than once. You can also make muffins and small loaves using this recipe; bake for 30 to 35 minutes."

INGREDIENTS

3 cups canned pumpkin puree

$1^{1}/_{2}$ cups vegetable oil

4 cups white sugar

6 eggs

$4^{3}/_{4}$ cups all-purpose flour

$1^{1}/_{2}$ teaspoons baking powder

$1^{1}/_{2}$ teaspoons baking soda

$1^{1}/_{2}$ teaspoons salt

$1^{1}/_{2}$ teaspoons ground cinnamon

$1^{1}/_{2}$ teaspoons ground nutmeg

$1^{1}/_{2}$ teaspoons ground cloves

DIRECTIONS

1. Preheat the oven to 350°F (175°C). Grease and flour three 9x5 inch loaf pans.

2. In a large bowl, mix together the pumpkin, oil, sugar, and eggs. Combine the flour, baking powder, baking soda, salt, cinnamon, nutmeg, and cloves; stir into the pumpkin mixture until well blended. Divide the batter evenly between the prepared pans.

3. Bake in preheated oven for 45 minutes to 1 hour. The top of the loaf should spring back when lightly pressed.

Pumpkin Pie Bread

Submitted by: **Tanja Miller**

Makes: 2 - 9x5 inch loaves

Preparation: 15 minutes

Cooking: 1 hour

Ready In: 1 hour 15 minutes

"This quick bread recipe tastes like pumpkin pie. Tastes best when served the next day."

INGREDIENTS

3¹/₂ cups all-purpose flour

2 teaspoons baking soda

1 teaspoon baking powder

3 teaspoons pumpkin pie spice

1 teaspoon salt

3 cups white sugar

1 cup vegetable oil

4 eggs

1 (15 ounce) can pumpkin puree

¹/₂ cup water

DIRECTIONS

1. Preheat oven to 350°F (175°C). Grease two 9x5 inch loaf pans. Sift together the flour, baking soda, baking powder, salt, and pumpkin pie spice. Set aside.

2. In a large bowl, beat together sugar, oil, eggs, and pumpkin. Stir in flour mixture alternately with water. Divide batter evenly between the prepared pans.

3. Bake in the preheated oven for 60 to 70 minutes, or until a toothpick inserted into the center comes out clean. For best flavor, store wrapped in plastic wrap at room temperature for a full day before serving.

Persimmon Bread II

Submitted by: **Nancy Scott**

Makes: 3 - 6x3 inch loaves

Preparation: 10 minutes

Cooking: 1 hour

Ready In: 1 hour 10 minutes

"Excellent for Christmas gifts, as persimmons are only available for a brief time. Moist spice cake type bread. This is the top seller at our company bake sale at Christmas!"

INGREDIENTS

1 cup persimmon pulp

2 teaspoons baking soda

3 cups white sugar

1 cup vegetable oil

4 eggs

1 1/2 teaspoons ground cinnamon

1/2 teaspoon ground nutmeg

1 1/2 teaspoons salt

2/3 cup water

3 cups all-purpose flour

1 cup chopped walnuts

DIRECTIONS

1. Preheat the oven to 350°F (175°C). Grease three 6x3 inch loaf pans.

2. In a small bowl, stir together the persimmon pulp and baking soda. Let stand 5 minutes to thicken the pulp.

3. In a medium bowl, combine sugar, oil, eggs, cinnamon, nutmeg, and salt. Blend until smooth. Mix in persimmon pulp and water alternately with flour. Fold in nuts. Divide batter into the prepared pans, filling each pan 2/3 full.

4. Bake for 1 hour in the preheated oven, or until a toothpick inserted comes out clean. Cool in pan for 10 minutes before removing to a wire rack to cool completely.

Chocolate Chip Pumpkin Bread

Submitted by: **Star Pooley**

Makes: 3 - loaf pans

Preparation: 30 minutes

Cooking: 1 hour

Ready In: 1 hour 30 minutes

"I make this recipe during the holidays. It is moist, and freezes well! I bake them in coffee cans, and wrap them in colored cellophane to give as gifts."

INGREDIENTS

3 cups white sugar

1 (15 ounce) can pumpkin puree

1 cup vegetable oil

2/3 cup water

4 eggs

3 1/2 cups all-purpose flour

1 tablespoon ground cinnamon

1 tablespoon ground nutmeg

2 teaspoons baking soda

1 1/2 teaspoons salt

1 cup miniature semisweet chocolate chips

1/2 cup chopped walnuts (optional)

DIRECTIONS

1. Preheat oven to 350°F (175°C). Grease and flour three 1 pound size coffee cans, or three 9x5 inch loaf pans.

2. In a large bowl, combine sugar, pumpkin, oil, water, and eggs. Beat until smooth. Blend in flour, cinnamon, nutmeg, baking soda, and salt. Fold in chocolate chips and nuts. Fill cans ½ to ¾ full.

3. Bake for 1 hour, or until an inserted knife comes out clean. Cool on wire racks before removing from cans or pans.

Eggnog Quick Bread

Submitted by: **Mary E. Crain**

Makes: 1 - 9x5 inch loaf

Preparation: 10 minutes

Cooking: 1 hour

Ready In: 1 hour 10 minutes

"This cake gets better with age. It tastes like Christmas! Smaller loaves make excellent gifts. Use fresh eggnog, not the canned stuff."

INGREDIENTS

2 eggs

1 cup white sugar

1/2 cup butter, melted

1 cup eggnog

2 teaspoons rum flavored extract

1 teaspoon vanilla extract

2 1/4 cups all-purpose flour

2 teaspoons baking powder

1/2 teaspoon salt

1/4 teaspoon ground nutmeg

DIRECTIONS

1. Preheat oven to 350°F (175°C). Grease bottom only of a 9x5 inch loaf pan, or three 6x3 inch loaf pans.

2. Beat eggs in large bowl. Stir in sugar, melted butter, eggnog, rum extract, and vanilla. Combine the flour, baking powder, salt, and nutmeg. Stir into eggnog mixture, just enough to moisten dry ingredients. Pour batter into prepared pan or pans.

3. Bake bread in large pan for 40 to 60 minutes, or until a toothpick inserted in the center comes out clean. Breads baked in the smaller pans require 25 to 40 minutes. Let cool in pan for 10 minutes, then turn out onto a wire rack, and cool completely. Wrap tightly, and store in the refrigerator.

Boiled Fruitcake

Submitted by: **Mark Richards**

Makes: 1 - 8 inch cake

Preparation: 20 minutes

Cooking: 2 hours 10 minutes

Ready In: 2 hours 40 minutes

"This recipe produces a really moist fruitcake. It was given to me by my mom, and it's really easy. My mom uses it for Christmas cake by icing it. I use it for birthdays, Christmas, or just for a treat. If mixed spice is unavailable, substitute with a pinch each of cinnamon, coriander, cloves, nutmeg, and ginger."

INGREDIENTS

2 cups chopped dried mixed fruit

1 cup roughly chopped glace cherries

1/4 cup candied mixed citrus peel

1/2 cup chopped walnuts

1 1/2 cups white sugar

3/4 cup butter

1 cup milk

1 teaspoon mixed spice

1/2 teaspoon baking soda

2 2/3 cups sifted self-rising flour

2 eggs

DIRECTIONS

1. Preheat oven to 325°F (160°C). Line one 8x3 inch round cake tin with parchment paper.

2. In a medium saucepan, combine mixed fruit, cherries, citrus peel, walnuts, sugar, butter, milk, mixed spice, and baking soda. Bring to a boil, and simmer for 5 minutes. Let the mixture cool to room temperature.

3. Stir in flour and eggs. Pour into the prepared pan. Wrap outside of pan with brown paper or newspaper.

4. Bake at 325°F (160°C) for 40 minutes, then reduce temperature to 300°F (150°C), and continue to baking cake for 1½ hours. Remove cake from oven, and allow to cool in the tin for 5 minutes, then turn it out onto a cooling rack, remove paper, and cool completely. Cake can be stored for up to 6 months wrapped in foil and in an airtight tin.

Christmas Fruitcake

Submitted by: **Karen Uffelman**

Makes: 1 - 6 inch round pan

Preparation: 20 minutes

Cooking: 45 minutes

Ready In: 10 weeks

"It's a shame that fruitcake as a species gets such a bad rap. With its two key ingredients - rum and butter - it ought to be a hit. This recipe is less dense and more cake-like than many fruitcake recipes. It has become a favorite of my friends and family around the holidays (even the skeptical ones), and is delicious by itself, or covered with a layer of almond paste."

INGREDIENTS

1/8 cup chopped dried cherries

1/8 cup chopped dried mango

1/4 cup dried cranberries

1/4 cup currants

2 tablespoons chopped candied citron

1/4 cup dark rum

1/2 cup butter

1/4 cup packed brown sugar

1 egg

1/2 cup all-purpose flour

1/8 teaspoon baking soda

1/4 teaspoon salt

1/4 teaspoon ground cinnamon

1/4 cup unsulfured molasses

2 tablespoons milk

1/4 cup chopped pecans

1/4 cup dark rum, divided

DIRECTIONS

1. Soak cherries, mango, cranberries, currants, and citron in 1/4 cup rum for at least 24 hours. Cover tightly, and store at room temperature.

2. Preheat oven to 325°F (165°C). Butter a 6x3 inch round pan, and line with parchment paper.

3. In a large bowl, cream together butter and brown sugar until fluffy. Beat in egg. Whisk together flour, baking soda, salt, and cinnamon; mix into butter and sugar in three batches, alternating with molasses and milk. Stir in soaked fruit and chopped nuts. Scrape batter into prepared pan.

4. Bake in preheated oven for 40 to 45 minutes. Cool in the pan for 10 minutes, then sprinkle with 2 tablespoons rum.

5. Cut out one piece parchment paper and one piece cheesecloth, each large enough to wrap around the cake. Moisten cheesecloth with 1 tablespoon rum. Arrange cheesecloth on top of parchment paper, and unmold cake onto it. Sprinkle top and sides of cake with remaining rum. Wrap the cheesecloth closely to the surface of the cake, then wrap with paper. Place in an airtight tin, and age for at least 10 weeks. If storing longer, douse with additional rum for every 10 weeks of storage.

Christmas Cake

Submitted by: **Carol**

Makes: 1 - 8 inch square fruit cake
Preparation: 30 minutes
Cooking: 3 hours 30 minutes
Ready In: 6 hours

"This cake is a rich, dark, moist fruit cake, very flavorful at Christmas. Try icing with almond paste for a more festive touch. This recipe is started in October or November so as to let it mellow before the holidays. I remember very well my mother storing her fruit cake in an old butter churn that belonged to my grand-mother and great grandmother. I wish that I had that old crock."

INGREDIENTS

2 (8 ounce) containers candied cherries

1 (8 ounce) container candied mixed citrus peel

2 cups raisins

1 cup currants

1 cup dates, pitted and chopped

2 (2.25 ounce) packages blanched slivered almonds

1/2 cup brandy

1/2 cup all-purpose flour

2 cups all-purpose flour

1/2 teaspoon baking soda

1 teaspoon ground cloves

1 teaspoon ground allspice

1 teaspoon ground cinnamon

1/2 teaspoon salt

1 cup butter

2 cups packed brown sugar

6 eggs

3/4 cup molasses

3/4 cup apple juice

DIRECTIONS

1. In a medium bowl, combine cherries, citrus peel, raisins, currants, dates, and almonds. Stir in brandy; let stand 2 hours, or overnight. Dredge soaked fruit with ½ cup flour.

2. Preheat oven to 275°F (135°C). Grease an 8x8x3 inch fruit cake pan, line with parchment paper, and grease again. In a small bowl, mix together 2 cups flour, baking soda, cloves, allspice, cinnamon, and salt; set aside.

3. In a large bowl, cream butter until light. Gradually blend in brown sugar and eggs. Mix together molasses and apple juice. Beat into butter mixture alternately with flour mixture, making 4 dry and 3 liquid additions. Fold in floured fruit. Turn batter into prepared pan.

4. Bake in preheated oven for 3 to 3½ hours, or until a toothpick inserted into the center of cake comes out clean. Remove from pan, and lift off paper. Cool cake completely, then wrap loosely in waxed paper. Store in an airtight container.

Dawn's Candied Walnuts

Submitted by: **Dawn Timmerman**

Makes: 1 pound

Preparation: 10 minutes

Cooking: 20 minutes

Ready In: 30 minutes

"These walnuts are a special treat for Christmas, and are well worth the time it takes to make them."

INGREDIENTS

1 pound walnut halves

1 cup white sugar

2 teaspoons ground cinnamon

$1/4$ teaspoon salt

6 tablespoons milk

1 teaspoon vanilla extract

DIRECTIONS

1. Preheat oven to 350°F (175°C). Spread nuts in a single layer over a baking sheet. Roast for approximately 8 to 10 minutes, or until the nuts start to turn brown and the smell of roasting nuts fills the kitchen.

2. Stir together sugar, cinnamon, salt, and milk in a medium saucepan. Cook over medium-high heat for 8 minutes, or until the mixture reaches the soft ball stage of 236°F (113°C). Remove from heat, and stir in vanilla immediately.

3. Add walnuts to sugar syrup, and stir to coat well. Spoon nuts onto waxed paper, and immediately separate nuts with a fork. Cool, and store in airtight containers.

Glazed Nuts

Submitted by: **Rosemary**

Makes: 1 pound

Preparation: 15 minutes

Cooking: 30 minutes

Ready In: 45 minutes

"Glazed nuts are a favorite holiday snack, and are very simple to make. Use walnuts, pecans, almonds, or a mix."

INGREDIENTS

1 egg white

1/2 cup packed brown sugar

2 tablespoons ground cinnamon

1 teaspoon ground cloves

1 teaspoon ground ginger

1 tablespoon vanilla extract

1 pound walnut halves

DIRECTIONS

1. Preheat oven to 300°F (150°C). Coat a baking sheet with cooking spray.

2. In a large bowl, beat egg white until foamy. Stir in brown sugar, cinnamon, cloves, ginger, and vanilla. Add nuts, and stir to coat. Spread evenly onto prepared pan.

3. Bake for 30 minutes, stirring occasionally, or until well toasted and golden brown. Remove from oven, and cool completely. Store in an airtight container.

Swedish Nuts

Submitted by: **Barbara Sheehan**

Makes: 4 cups

Preparation: 10 minutes

Cooking: 40 minutes

Ready In: 50 minutes

"These are delicious. My friends all now eagerly expect them for Christmas. They are perfect for holiday gifts!"

INGREDIENTS

3 1/2 cups mixed nuts

1/2 cup butter

2 egg whites

1 cup white sugar

salt to taste

DIRECTIONS

1. Preheat oven to 325°F (165°C).

2. Place nuts on a 10x15 inch jellyroll pan, and bake for 10 minutes. Remove nuts, and melt butter on pan.

3. In a medium bowl, beat egg whites until soft peaks form. Gradually beat in the sugar and salt. Fold toasted nuts into egg white mixture. Arrange the coated nuts in a single layer on the buttered pan.

4. Bake for 30 minutes in the preheated oven, turning nuts with spatula every 10 minutes, until outside is crisp and golden. Cool, and store in an airtight container.

Cinnamon-Roasted Almonds

Submitted by: **BJ**

Makes: 4 cups

Preparation: 15 minutes

Cooking: 1 hour

Ready In: 1 hour 15 minutes

"Here is an easy snack idea to serve at any holiday party."

INGREDIENTS

1 egg white

1 teaspoon cold water

4 cups whole almonds

1/2 cup white sugar

1/4 teaspoon salt

1/2 teaspoon ground cinnamon

DIRECTIONS

1. Preheat oven to 250°F (120°C). Lightly grease a 10x15 inch jellyroll pan.

2. Lightly beat the egg white; add water, and beat until frothy but not stiff. Add the nuts, and stir until well coated. Mix the sugar, salt, and cinnamon, and sprinkle over the nuts. Toss to coat, and spread evenly on the prepared pan.

3. Bake for 1 hour in the preheated oven, stirring occasionally, until golden. Allow to cool, then store nuts in airtight containers.

Cappuccino in a Jar

Submitted by: **Cindy**

Makes: 2 - 12 ounce jars

Preparation: 10 minutes

Ready In: 10 minutes

"Cappuccino mix that can be placed in a jar. It makes a great gift to go along with cookies in a jar! It could also be used in a fundraiser."

INGREDIENTS

2/3 cup instant coffee granules

1 cup powdered non-dairy creamer

1 cup powdered chocolate drink mix

1/2 cup white sugar

3/4 teaspoon ground cinnamon

3/8 teaspoon ground nutmeg

DIRECTIONS

1. Have ready 2 (12 ounce) canning jars. Put the instant coffee into a food processor, and process to a fine powder. If you don't have a food processor, put it into a large plastic bag, and crush with a rolling pin.

2. In a large bowl, combine creamer, chocolate mix, instant coffee, sugar, cinnamon, and nutmeg. Stir together until well mixed. Spoon into 2 - 12 ounce jars.

3. Attach a note to each jar that reads:

   CAPPUCCINO:

   Mix 3 tablespoons of powder with 6 fluid ounces hot water.

Hot Cocoa Mix in a Jar

Submitted by: **Traci (TJ)**

Makes: 8 cups of mix

Preparation: 10 minutes

Ready In: 10 minutes

"We take this to Holiday parties and on camping trips. Dress up the jar, and it makes a great Holiday gift."

INGREDIENTS

6¹/₂ cups powdered milk

1 (5 ounce) package non-instant chocolate pudding mix

1 cup powdered chocolate drink mix

¹/₂ cup powdered non-dairy creamer

¹/₂ cup confectioners' sugar

¹/₂ cup unsweetened cocoa powder

DIRECTIONS

1. In a large bowl, combine powdered milk, chocolate pudding mix, chocolate drink mix powder, creamer, confectioners' sugar, and cocoa. Divide the mixture between two 1 quart jars. Seal, and decorate as desired. These can be stored in a dry area for up to 3 months.

2. Attach a tag with the following instructions:

   HOT COCOA:

   Dissolve a cup cocoa mix in 1 cup boiling water.

Chocolate Cookie Mix in a Jar

Submitted by: **Jennifer**

Makes: 3 dozen

Preparation: 25 minutes

Ready In: 25 minutes

"This is a great Christmas or birthday gift. Everybody loves to bake, yet no one has the time. It is a thoughtful gift for the busy person in your life. And by the way, the cookies are delicious!"

INGREDIENTS

1³/4 cups all-purpose flour

1 teaspoon baking powder

1 teaspoon baking soda

1/4 teaspoon salt

3/4 cup dark brown sugar

1/2 cup white sugar

1/4 cup cocoa

1/2 cup chopped pecans

1 cup semi-sweet chocolate chips

DIRECTIONS

1. Combine all-purpose flour, baking powder, baking soda, and salt. Set aside.

2. In a 1 quart wide mouth canning jar, layer dark brown sugar, white sugar, cocoa, chopped pecans, and chocolate chips. Pack everything down firmly before you add flour mixture, it will be a snug fit.

3. Attach a tag with the following instructions:

   CHOCOLATE COOKIE MIX IN A JAR:

   1. Preheat oven to 350°F (175°C)

   2. Empty cookie mix into large bowl. Thoroughly blend mixture with hands. Mix in ¾ cup softened butter or margarine, 1 egg, slightly beaten, and 1 teaspoon vanilla. Shape into walnut size balls, and place 2 inches apart on a parchment lined baking sheet.

   3. Bake for 11 to 13 minutes. Cool 5 minutes on baking sheet, then move to wire racks.

Snickerdoodle Mix in a Jar

Submitted by: **Diane**

Makes: 3 dozen

Preparation: 15 minutes

Ready In: 15 minutes

"Another 'cookie mix in a jar' recipe for the collection."

INGREDIENTS

2³/₄ cups all-purpose flour

¹/₄ teaspoon salt

1 teaspoon baking soda

2 teaspoons cream of tartar

1¹/₂ cups white sugar

DIRECTIONS

1. In a large bowl, combine the flour, salt, baking soda, cream of tartar, and sugar. Stir with a whisk, then place into a one quart canning jar.

2. Attach a tag with the following recipe to the jar:

   SNICKERDOODLES

   1. Preheat oven to 350°F (175°C).

   2. In a large bowl, cream 1 cup of butter and 2 eggs. Pour in the snickerdoodle mix, and stir until a dough forms. In a small bowl, combine ½ cup of sugar and 1 tablespoon of cinnamon. Roll the dough into 1 inch balls, roll the balls in the cinnamon-sugar mixture, and place 2 inches apart on an ungreased cookie sheet.

   3. Bake for 10 to 15 minutes in the preheated oven. Cookies should be light brown. Cool on wire racks.

Cranberry Hootycreeks

Submitted by: **Susan O'Dell**

Makes: 18 cookies

Preparation: 25 minutes

Ready In: 25 minutes

"A beautifully festive cookie in a jar recipe. These make great gifts."

INGREDIENTS

5/8 cup all-purpose flour

1/2 cup rolled oats

1/2 cup all-purpose flour

1/2 teaspoon baking soda

1/2 teaspoon salt

1/3 cup packed brown sugar

1/3 cup white sugar

1/2 cup dried cranberries

1/2 cup white chocolate chips

1/2 cup chopped pecans

DIRECTIONS

1. Layer the ingredients in a 1 quart or 1 liter jar, in the order listed.

2. Attach a tag with the following instructions:

CRANBERRY HOOTYCREEKS

1. Preheat oven to 350°F (175°C). Grease a cookie sheet or line with parchment paper.

2. In a medium bowl, beat together ½ cup softened butter, 1 egg and 1 teaspoon of vanilla until fluffy. Add the entire jar of ingredients, and mix together by hand until well blended. Drop by heaping spoonfuls onto the prepared baking sheets.

3. Bake for 8 to 10 minutes, or until edges start to brown. Cool on baking sheets, or remove to cool on wire racks.

Friendship Soup Mix in a Jar

Submitted by: **Bea**

Makes: 16 servings

Preparation: 30 minutes

Cooking: 1 hour

Ready In: 1 hour 30 minutes

"Your friends and family will love you for this! A soup mix in a jar recipe you can give out as gifts!"

INGREDIENTS

¹/₂ cup dry split peas

¹/₃ cup beef bouillon granules

¹/₄ cup pearl barley

¹/₂ cup dry lentils

¹/₄ cup dried onion flakes

2 teaspoons dried Italian seasoning

¹/₂ cup uncooked long grain rice

2 bay leaves

¹/₂ cup uncooked alphabet pasta

DIRECTIONS

1. In a 1½ pint jar, layer the split peas, bouillon, barley, lentils, onion flakes, Italian seasoning, rice, and bay leaves. Wrap the pasta in plastic wrap, and place in the jar. Seal tightly.

2. Attach a label to the jar with the following instructions:

   FRIENDSHIP SOUP

   ADDITIONAL INGREDIENTS:
   1 pound ground beef, black pepper to taste, garlic powder to taste, 1 (28 ounce) can diced tomatoes - undrained, 1 (6 ounce) can tomato paste, and 3 quarts water.

   TO PREPARE SOUP:
   Remove pasta from top of jar, and set aside. In a large pot over medium heat, brown beef with pepper and garlic; drain excess fat. Add diced tomatoes, tomato paste, water, and soup mix. Bring to a boil, then reduce heat to low. Cover, and simmer for 45 minutes. Stir in the pasta, cover, and simmer 15 to 20 minutes, or until the pasta, peas, lentils and barley are tender.

recipe contributors

index

credits

the staff at allrecipes

Jennifer Anderson
Kala Anderson
Karen Anderson
Barbara Antonio
Emily Brune
Scotty Carreiro
Sydny Carter
Jill Charing
Jeff Cummings
Kirk Dickinson
Steven Hamilton
Blanca Hernandez
Tim Hunt

Richard Kozel
William Marken
Wendy McKay
Elana Miller
Carrie Mills
Bill Moore
Todd Moore
Yann Oehl
Alicia Power
Judy St. John
Britt Swearingen
Esmee Williams
Krista Winjum

thanks

The staff would like to thank the following people whose comments and feedback have made this a better book: Brenda Hunt, David Quinn, and Hillary Quinn.

the allrecipes tried & true series

Our *Tried & True* cookbooks feature the very best recipes from the world's greatest home cooks! Allrecipes.com, the #1 recipe website, brings you the "Best of the Best" dishes and treats, selected from over 24,000 recipes! We hand-picked only recipes that have been awarded 5-star ratings time and time again, so you know every dish is a winner.

Current titles include:

Allrecipes Tried & True Favorites; Top 300 Recipes

Filled with the best-loved recipes from Allrecipes.com - these have all won repeated standing ovations from millions of home cooks and their families, intrepid eaters and picky kids alike.

Allrecipes Tried & True Cookies; Top 200 Recipes

Enjoy the world's best cookie recipes and invaluable baking tips and tricks that will turn anyone into an expert on preparing, decorating and sharing cookies. With over 230 cookie recipes, you'll find tried and true recipes for all your old favorites, and lots of new favorites too!

Allrecipes Tried & True - Quick & Easy; Top 200 Recipes

Great-tasting meals in minutes! This cookbook features delicious dishes that can be prepared in minutes. Discover the joys of cooking without spending hours in the kitchen!

Allrecipes Tried & True - Slow Cooker & Casserole; Top 200 Recipes

Within the pages of this cookbook you'll find recipes for exceptional casseroles and slow cooker that offer the best in both convenience and crowd-pleasing flavors, just right for weeknight dinners, potlucks and family gatherings.

Allrecipes Tried & True - All Season Grilling & BBQ; Top 200 Recipes

America's best-loved grilling and barbeque recipes have been pulled together for this one-of-a-kind collection featuring Allrecipes best-of-the-best recipes for sizzling steaks, juicy chicken, sensational seafood, zesty sauces and marinades, simple salads, side dishes and more.

Allrecipes *Tried & True* cookbooks are available at select bookstores, by visiting our website at http://www.allrecipes.com, or by calling 206-292-3990 ext. #0. Watch for more *Tried & True* cookbooks to come!

Allrecipes.com · 3317 3rd Ave S., Suite D · Seattle, WA 98134 USA · Phone: (206) 292-3990